THE DIPLOMACY OF
THE 'NEW ORDER'

ARTHUR STAM

THE DIPLOMACY OF THE 'NEW ORDER'

The Foreign Policy of Japan, Germany and Italy: 1931-1945

2003 ASPEKT

The diplomacy of the 'New Order'.
© Arthur Stam
© 2003 Uitgeverij Aspekt bv
Amersfoortsestraat 27, 3769 AD Soesterberg, The Netherlands
aspekt@ision.nl / www.uitgeverijaspekt.nl
Cover design: Peter Koch
Inside: Van Swieten & Partner, Nieuwegein, The Netherlands
ISBN: 90-5911-436-1

All rights reserved. No part of this publication may be reproduced in any form or by any means without the written permission of the publisher.

Contents

Introduction 7
Rebellious chauvinism 9
Aggression through insubordination 12
Manchukuo and the League of Nations 14
On the way to the Anti-Comintern Pact 16
The implications of the Anti-Comintern Pact 19
The axis Rome-Berlin 22
Germany and the Japanese-Chinese war 26
The 'Pact of Steel' 32
Japan and the Stalin-Hitler-pact 35
Italy: from non-belligerence towards intervention 40
The realisation of the Tripartite Pact 47
The extension of the Tripartite Pact 51
Between Barbarossa and Pearl Harbor 60
Between Pearl Harbor and Stalingrad 78
On the way to the end 89
The conclusion of Bernd Wegner 105
Bibliography 107
Register 110

Introduction

Japan, Germany and Italy had a lot in common since 1933, both ideologically and strategically. Their ideology professed a myth that justified their aggressive expansion. As far as their interests were concerned, all three of them were hostile towards the nations that were in the way of the expansion of the *Drei Habenichtse* (the three countries who had nothing), the USSR and the western democracies. Besides these similarities there were also major differences, regarding their fundamentals and interests, between the nations that formed this 'New Order'. For example, Japan did not have a charismatic leader like *Il Duce* or *Der Führer*. As far as their interests were concerned, all three of them were inclined to operate on their own. The best example of this is their relation with the USSR. In 1936 Japan and Germany concluded their Anti-Comintern Pact, but that really did not mean much in the diplomatic reality of those days. When in 1937 war broke out between Japan and China, Japan used it to start a crusade against communism, while Germany continued to support the Chinese war activities until 1938. In August 1939 Germany concluded a non-aggression pact with the USSR, which was a major violation of their commitments towards Japan. This happened at a moment, coinciding with heavy fighting between troops of the USSR and Japan; on the border of Moscow's oldest satellite state, the People's Republic of Mongolia and Tokyo's satellite-empire, Manchukuo. After Germany invaded the USSR in 1941, Japan did nothing. In 1942 and 1943 the Japanese and Italian governments tried in vain to convince Germany to make peace with the USSR, because they wanted to concentrate the German war potential against the western Allies.

The Tripartite Pact, dating from September 1940, was mainly directed against the United States. It resulted, after the surprise attack of Japan on Pearl Harbor, in the German declaration of war against the United States. Both The Anti-Comintern Pact as well as the Tripartite Pact was expanded with the regimes of small nations. Since 1941 these treaties had a lot more meaning in Europe than in eastern Asia, mainly because of the behaviour of Japan.

The diplomacy of the three powers became more complicated as a result of the heterogeneity of their governments, which at best can be characterised as authoritarian pluralism. That resulted in struggles of competency within the establishment, what especially had its effects on the policy of Japan. The reason for taking Japan as a starting point is purely chronological. The history of the Second World War started in the Far East. This view, which is obvious to me, deviates from the conventional view of seeing the German invasion of Poland in September 1939 as the beginning of the Second World War. As a result of this the war in Europe started, at a moment a Japanese-Chinese war had been going on for over two years already. While it is surely possible to consider Hitler's rise to power (1933) as the prelude to the war in Europe, the prologue of the Japanese war against China and the United States started with the occupation of Manchuria in 1931. Only in December 1941, after the surprise attack of Japan on Pearl Harbor, the European war and the escalating Japanese-Chinese war resulted in a real World War. Therefore, I do not view the Nazi takeover of power as the beginning, but the Japanese aggression against Manchuria, which gave a decisive push in the direction of the New Order. That New Order could be presented as a *Schicksalgemeinschaft* (community of destiny) after all three future allies announced a severe disturbance of the status quo by leaving the League of Nations.

Rebellious chauvinism

In Japan the emperor was considered to be of divine descent. As a result of that, he was formally elevated above the various parties of power that determined policy. The decision making process was painful, especially as a result of the rivalry between the army and the navy. Although emperor Hirohito was in a position to act as a supreme referee, both during and after World War Two, he hardly availed himself of that option.

Within the framework of his high position it was decided, in 1928, to absolve him from any responsibilities regarding official government policies. That was the case as far it concerned civilian politicians. Their distance towards the throne was advantageous for the military leaders, who had the right of direct access to the emperor. This situation gave some of the generals the opportunity to pretend they were speaking in the name of the emperor and impose their will on the government. Their policies, however, were largely dependent on imperial approval. Navy and army had to ask his permission for their plans of action.

He informally influenced the details of the plans that were drawn up, usually through the high officers who had an audience with him. In most cases he approved the ideas of his commanding officers but in some instances – as we will see later on – he intervened to set another course of action. Besides, at some times he reacted quite sharply against officers who had too much a mind of their own. This became a serious problem. Around 1930 there were some army units, believing the establishment was much too tame, consequently going their own aggressive way.

During World War One Japan had taken advantage of the fact that the major allied powers were fully absorbed by their warfare on the European continent. Therefore the Japanese authorities were in a position to put China under their guardianship and occupy the naval base of Vladivostok, taking advantage of the chaotic plight of Russia in eastern Siberia. This imperialistic performance was annulled when the United States had their hands free after the war. It boiled down to a shift of power, imposed during the Washington Conference (1920-1921). By virtue of the Nine-Power Pact, the sovereignty of China was restored, which also included the restoration of the 'open door' (free access and equal opportunity). The treaty stated that Japan was allowed to possess a tonnage of warships up to a maximum of three-fifth of the tonnage that was secured by the United States and Great Britain together. In 1930 this was expanded as a result of the Treaty of London, which meant the same rules applied regarding their fleet of submarines. Six weeks later Japanese Prime Minister Hamaguchi was murdered. The young killer was an exponent of the nationalistic resistance against the naval treaty.

Vladivostok, the harbour — an important target of the Japanese expansion.

He experienced a lot of sympathy for his action in the Japanese press. There were also various other activities organised in support of him. It became popular, because between 1930 and 1936, various politicians who failed in their role as 'hurrah patriots', were murdered.

These were the symptoms of a rebellious chauvinism, which was being strengthened by the economic depression that shocked the world since 1929. These were difficult times for the farmers as a result of lower prices for rice and silk, while the amounts they had to pay for rent and taxes remained equal. Because most of the soldiers and lower ranked officers came from the country, it resulted in social unrest within the army. That was also based on the conviction that the establishment was too weak to serve the national interests. The discriminating immigration policy of the United States and barriers against export from Japan would leave no other option than expansion, according to the ideologists of a national discomfort. This feeling also took hold of the high ranked officers. Consequently the Japanese aggression in the thirties – that began as ventures as a result of insubordination – turned out to be supported by a majority of the establishment.

Aggression through insubordination
Between World War One and the end of the twenties China lacked a central authority. The country was divided between warlords. This situation came more or less to an end when the military leader of the 'Kuomintang' (National People's Party), Chiang Kai-shek, completed his successful march to the north. By 1928 most of the warlords had fled for him. In Manchuria, warlord Chang Tso-lin, who acted as a somewhat recalcitrant satellite of Japan, was still in power. This special position of Japan was mainly based on the South-Manchurian Railroad. It formed an exterritorial complex, which also consisted of mines, power plants and warehouses. And in the south there was the peninsula of Kwangtung (formerly called Liaotung), which gave its name to the Japanese Kwangtung army in Southern Manchuria. It was here where the military adventures started, which were so characteristic for Japan in the thirties.

The prelude started in 1928 when colonel Komoto, without knowledge of his superiors, had warlord Chang Tso-lin murdered. With this action he hoped to create the chaos, which would give the Kwangtung army the necessary excuse to restore order, in other words to take over Manchuria. Mainly as a result of the restrained reaction of the local Chinese authorities it turned out differently. Prime Minister Tanaka wanted to take disciplinary action against Komoto and his accomplices, but this fell through as a result of opposition from the Ministry of War. Subsequently, emperor Hirohito impelled the tormented Prime Minister to resign. The murder resulted in an opposite effect as the son and successor of Chang Tso-lin, Chang Hsueh-liang, joined the Kuomintang. In other words, it ended the role of this warlord as a satellite of Japan. This gave an additional incentive to the subversive elements in the Kwangtung army to seize the opportunity. They felt that Manchuria, rich in minerals, fertile and sparsely populated, had to be conquered to allow the settlement of a part of the Japanese surplus population.

In 1931, on September 18, an explosion occurred at Mukden on the South Manchurian Railroad, which destroyed a major part of the tracks. Two officers of the Kwangtung army, lieutenant-colonel Itagaki and captain Ishiwara, had staged it. The bomb attack was attributed to the Chinese troops, after which units of the Kwangtung answered by opening fire.

It was only after all this had happened, that Itagaki informed the commander of the Kwangtung army, general Hojo. Subsequently, Japanese troops from Korea, on their own, also invaded Manchuria. Soon after, Manchuria was fully occupied, which made the Japanese government decide to join in with the unauthorised actions of their military. Although the emperor approved of their actions afterwards, he tried to get a better grip on the military from now on. The generals and admirals were forced to consult Hirohito more often. It did not turn out to be a great success, as the events of 1937 would show; the real war that broke out with China at that time was initiated by local commanding officers, who initially did not care too much about the opinions of their superiors.

Manchukuo and the League of Nations

In December 1931, the newly installed Japanese government hesitantly joined in with the accomplished facts of the events that had taken place in Manchuria. That applied especially to the minister of war Araki, who was very popular among radical young officers. Chang Hsueh-liang retreated from Manchuria with all of his troops, which meant that nothing of the Kwangtung regime was left behind. The American Secretary of State, Stimson, came up with a doctrine that bears his name; the Unites States would not recognise a change in the status quo that would affect the sovereignty of China and the 'open door', even if Japan would impose an agreement on China covering this topic. The Stimson doctrine has become the term for the non-recognition of changes in a country's borders, which have been realised as a result of aggression.

In February and March 1932, the Kwangtung army in Manchuria founded the satellite state of Manchukuo (the empire of the Manchus). Under heavy pressure Pu Yi, the former Chinese child emperor, became its governor for the time being. This resulted in a regime that could count on some native collaborators, but horrified the majority of the Chinese living there. It wasn't until six months later, in September, that this creation of the Kwangtung army was acknowledged by the Japanese government. In the meantime the Japanese Prime Minister Inukai, who aimed at reaching a compromise with China and didn't want to send any more troops, had been murdered.

Although the United States were not a member of the

Sadao Araki, popular among radical young officers.

League of Nations, Washington did get involved in their conferences. Based on the Lytton report on Manchuria, the Assembly of the League of Nations condemned the actions of Japan with 42 against 1 (Japan of course), which resulted in Japan leaving the League of Nations. There was also one abstention, of Siam, which became Thailand later on. This happened on February 27, 1933, when Hitler had been chancellor for almost a month. But at that moment the offices of Foreign Affairs and War were in the hands of the non-Nazi's von Neurath and Blomberg, which contributed in the first years of the Third Reich to the fact that the German-Chinese relations remained – as we will sketch out later on – quite good.

On the way to the Anti-Comintern Pact

The German approach to Japan, which was still quite isolated in 1933, was rather twisty. That was partly the fault of the Nazi's. Their theory on the superiority of the Nordic race was shocking for a proud and nationalistic people like the Japanese. That revealed itself in Hitler's *Mein Kampf*. In this book humanity was divided into three categories: 'creators of culture' (only the Nordic race!), 'bearers of culture' (for instance the Japanese) and 'destroyers of culture' (the Jews!). Hitler was of the opinion that the Japanese were an example of the category 'bearers of culture'. According to him, Japanese science and technology owed its status to the Arian influence. If that influence would no longer be there, Japan would decay into a plight of fossilisation. But in his major work *Der Führer* spotted something very positive about the Japanese. While the Jews did manage to succeed in undermining and bastardise the Europeans, the Japanese avoided that disaster because of their national pride and purity. It was for this reason that the 'British-Jewish' press, in its excitement over the empire of Japan and its militarism, prepared a war of destruction against this nation of islands in East Asia. In brief, the leader of the Third Reich thought the Japanese were brave and sympathetic, but certainly not equal. Nazi Germany understood this was annoying as it started to perceive a German-Japanese *Schicksalgemeinschaft* against Bolshevism and the western democracies. Especially the Foreign office, which until 1938 was not yet subject to the *Gleichschaltung* (complete nazification), warned for the dangers lurking behind this theory of race superiority. Nevertheless it was the Home Minister, the Nazi Frick, who argued in the *Ostasiatische Rundschau* of December 1933, that the German politics regarding race were not based on *Verschiedenwertigkeit* (superiority or inferiority) of the races but on its *Verschiedenartigkeit* (merely differences) and opposed miscegenation because of the latter. In his article he observed that the German opinions regarding race had caused anxiety in Asia, especially in Japan and British India. The *Aussenamt* (Foreign Office) was of opinion that Frick had not gone far enough and stated that any decision regarding race that would jeopardize Germany's foreign policy, would be avoided. Fricks solution to speak of disparity instead of inequality was followed by diplomats.

In 1934 a selection of Hitler's non-translated speeches was published in Tokyo by a professor in German. He had met Hitler in 1930. Hitler provided this anthology with an 'Introduction to the people of Japan'. It emphasized his appreciation for the fiery patriotism of the Japanese.

In those days the *Reichswehr* and the Foreign Office were not yet ready for diplomatic and strategic solidarity with Japan. This was overcome by the Nazi's by establishing a kind of parallel diplomacy; the so-called *Büro* or *Dienststelle* Ribbentrop, named after Hitler's diplomatic confidant and future Minister of Foreign Affairs. Excluding the Foreign Office, it laid the foundation for the Anti-Comintern Pact. In preparing the negotiations regarding this pact, Japan also excluded the Ministry of Foreign Affairs. They were part of the responsibilities of the military attaché of Japan in Berlin, Oshima, who was installed in the spring of 1934. He received instructions to find out what Germany would do in the case of a possible war

The diplomacy of the New Order, quite a complicated game of poker as shown by the Daily Mail.

between Japan and the USSR. Such an investigation did not appeal much to the Japanese Foreign Office. From the side of Germany they were also not yet ready for an alliance. Within the Ribbentrop bureau, the expert on the Far East, Von Raumer, looked for and found an unconventional alternative for a standard treaty. A protest by the United States with the USSR against the interference of the Communist International (Comintern) in US internal affairs provided him with the idea of the Anti-Comintern Pact in November 1935. He designed the treaty. Oshima and Ribbentrop agreed with it after a few alterations. But it still took a year before it was signed.

The idea of Von Raumer was also suitable to reassure

the *Wehrmacht* and the Foreign Office. When the German military attaché in Tokyo, Ott, got wind of the negotiations between Oshima and Ribbentrop, he warned his superiors against a military bond with Japan, which was too risky according to him. Minister Blomberg and chief of staff Beck supported his point of view. In addition, Ott informed the German ambassador in Tokyo, Von Dirksen, of the negotiations. When Von Dirksen was on leave in Germany, he interrogated Von Ribbentrop on this subject. Ribbentrop agreed that Von Dirksen would inform his Minister, Von Neurath. In Japan, in the meantime, the Foreign Office had also been brought in, as a result of which the Japanese ambassador in Berlin, Mushakoji, began to take part in the negotiations. In July 1936, Oshima caused a complication on behalf of the Japanese army command. He informed Von Raumer that the general staff of Japan wanted to include a clause regarding the question what one of the two partners would do or refrain from in case the other was attacked by the USSR. That idea did not appeal to Ribbentrop very much. A few days later the Civil War in Spain broke out, which intensified the anticommunist feelings of Hitler (and Mussolini). Hitler cordially welcomed Oshima and gave the green light to include the secret clauses requested by the Japanese generals. It took a few more months to complete the negotiations about them. On the 25th of November 1936 the treaty was solemnly signed by the two ambassadors: Mushakoji and Ribbentrop, who in the meantime had become ambassador in London.

The implications of the Anti-Comintern Pact
In the preamble, the subversive Comintern activities that

threatened world peace were mentioned, which made both nations decide on the following paragraphs:
1. Mutual information on the activities of the Comintern and consultation on the necessary measures that would have to be taken in close cooperation;
2. Common actions with other nations which were threatened by the subversive activities of the Comintern. These nations would be allowed to join the agreement;
3. Term of validity of five years.

An additional, non-secret, protocol provided for the establishment of a permanent committee that had to serve the objectives of the treaty. And there was the additional secret protocol, consisting of three paragraphs:
1. Committed the partners, that if one of them would be subject to an unprovoked attack or threat of attack by the USSR, the other party would refrain from any activities that would facilitate the position of the Soviet Union. (That did not mean much more than benevolent neutrality.);
2. None of them would sign a political treaty with the USSR, that went against the spirit of the pact and would be realised without mutual approval.
3. The protocol becomes effective simultaneously with the rest of the treaty and will be valid just as long.

There were rumours about secret clauses, of which the revelation by the Soviets about a secret offensive alliance topped everything. In reality the secret clauses were, as we have seen, rather weak. It is clear that in 1936 Japan stood more firm against the USSR than Germany; the Third

Von Ribbentrop.

Reich did not yet border the USSR, whereas Japan had come upon Soviet expansion on the North Chinese periphery. In 1921, Soviet intervention had led to a situation in which Outer Mongolia, since 1924 the People's Republic of Mongolia, became Moscow's first satellite state. In 1935 the USSR had given in to Japan by selling her railroad concession in Northern Manchuria to Manchukuo. Japan, in the meantime, had occupied Inner Mongolia. The USSR went after the confrontation with the Kwangtung army in 1932 by strengthening her armed forces in the Far East tremendously and by signing a treaty of mutual assistance with the People's Republic of Mongolia in 1936.

The geo-strategic difference between Japan and Germany was also expressed in the government proclamations that were made on the occasion of the treaty. In the Japanese document, people's attention was drawn to the communist forces that operated in China with support of the Soviet Union. The 'red aggression' against Outer Mongolia and Sinkiang (this region was also under Soviet influence) was also mentioned. Additionally it complained about the 7th Comintern Conference (1935), which according to Japan would boil down to an attempt to get control over all left wing movements. In the final paragraph it was claimed, that the Japanese government was looking 'to cooperate with as many nations possible'. The German document emphasised that the treaty was of a purely defensive nature and other nations that wanted to join would be very welcome. In the last sentence it was argued that 'the treaty would undoubtedly contribute towards world peace'.

The Japanese attempts to have Great Britain and The Netherlands join the treaty lead to nothing, whereas the Italian government was willing to join. The pact was not welcomed by the western democracies. They felt that the Japanese and German ambitions were aimed at the status quo in general.

The axis Rome-Berlin
The first two years after the *Machtsübernahme* (Hitler's rise to power), Italy and Germany did not get along very well.

In May 1934, the first meeting between *Il Duce* and *Der Führer*, in Venice, became a fiasco. Mussolini was left with a negative impression ('a dangerous dreamer') of his German colleague. A month and a half later that became even worse. The Nazi's attempted a coup in Austria that failed and during which chancellor Dolfuss, who was very close to Mussolini, was killed. To show that Italy would defend the independence of Austria even by force if necessary, Mussolini sent two army corps to the Brenner Pass. Hitler dissociated himself from this coup, which did not prevent the Italian press from overwhelming the German Reich with defamation. The Italian aggression against Abyssinia (Ethiopia) led to a reversal in their relations. After his performance at the Brenner-pass, Mussolini was of opinion that he was in high favour with Great Britain and especially France. He was partly wrong about that. In January 1935, Laval, the Minister of Foreign Affairs of France (and future collaborator) gave his approval to *Il Duce* for its campaign in the horn of Africa. (Later on the French minister claimed he only had approved Italy's economic penetration in Abyssinia, but that was implausible.) Also in Britain's government circles, the Italian annexation of Ethiopia was not considered to be unacceptable. The fact Mussolini partly miscalculated himself was based on underestimating the significance that an emotional public opinion can have in a democratic nation. Especially the outrage that developed in Great Britain made it necessary for the League of Nations to do something. That something was insufficient to bring the Italian aggression to a halt, but it was enough to cause a radical improvement in the German-Italian relations. A few days after the beginning of the Italian campaign, the League of Nations condemned this usurpation and proclaimed economic sanctions against Italy. These were not sufficient, especially because they did not include the supply of oil. In addition, Great Britain allowed the Italian maritime logistics, which were extremely vulnerable, to continue the use of the Suez Canal. In Italy the war was very popular. In May 1936 the Ethiopian capital Addis Abeba was conquered, after which the Italian king took on the title 'Emperor of Abyssinia'. The sanctions were subsequently cancelled.

Germany, which had left the League of Nations in October 1933 because of a deadlock on the subject of arms control, did not take part in the sanctions of course and offered Italy, after initially being neutral, economic support. In 1937 Italy followed the example of Japan and Germany by also leaving the League of Nations.

During the Abyssinian campaign, Hitler started with the remilitarisation of Rhineland, a violation of the Treaty of Locarno between Germany and the western Allies (1925), a risky but successful operation. In the meantime, a treaty signed in 1935 between France and the USSR on mutual assistance, had provided Germany an excuse to restore its unlimited military sovereignty. It underlined the fact that anticommunism did very well as a topic in the propaganda of the emerging New Order. That was brought out in full in 1936 by the start of the Spanish Civil War. Ignoring the farce of the so-called 'non intervention', Italy and Germany intervened on behalf of the Franco rebels, while the support of the Soviets to the Republicans, as far as manpower was concerned, was handled through the Comintern.

The 7th Comintern Conference (1935) had been dedicated to the topic of antifascist solidarity, the Popular Front.

Because of this, the Spanish Civil War, with her emotional international appeal, became a symbol of the fight between fascism and communism.

With regard to this civil war, a broad cooperation developed between Germany and Italy in the areas of diplomacy, ideology and the military. The lines of expansion did not cross each other, apart from the Balkan; Italy's ambitions concerned the Mediterranean, whereas Hitler's Germany was fully focused on its expansion to the East. The expansive temptations of Italy therefore, were more directed towards France, Great Britain and Yugoslavia than to the USSR. It meant that the partners of the Anti-Comintern Pact had ambitions that were not exclusively anti-communistic. When Italy joined the Anti-Comintern Pact in November 1937, the Italian Minister of Foreign Affairs, Ciano (also Mussolini's son-in-law), wrote in his diary that this treaty was mainly anti British. That was somewhat exaggerated. After all, Hitler was a virulent anticommunist and aspired a *modus vivendi* with Great Britain, while Japan operated under the flag of anticommunism, against China and the USSR, avoiding for the time being a hostile position towards the western democracies.

Albrecht Haushofer, son of the famous geo-politician, was at that time the representative of Ribbentrop in Japan. He informed his superior the Japanese were worried about the damage the Anti-Comintern Pact caused to the relations with Great Britain.

Because of all this, Italy acquired the status of junior partner within a few years. For example, in March 1938, Mussolini accepted the *Anschluss* of Austria with Germany unconditionally an annexation he regarded as unacceptable four years earlier. In October 1938, Italy also proclaimed a number of anti-Semitic laws, which excluded Jews from a number of professions. The Conference of Munich was held around the same time. It was during that meeting that the French and British governments, with mediation from Mussolini, gave in to the German demands regarding Czechoslovakia. The German annexation of Sudetenland, which had been completed, offered *Il Duce* some prestige. When Hitler and his gang, in March 1939, annexed Czechia and allowed Slovakia the status of satellite state, it meant the agreements of Munich were treated like a 'scrap of paper'. Mussolini, who was very vulnerable in his prestige feelings, was deeply hurt by this suddenly accomplished fact.

Germany and the Japanese-Chinese war

By 1927, the close relationship in China between the Kuomintang and the USSR had turned around. The Soviet-military delegation had to leave the country and was, not much later, replaced by German officers. Colonel Bauer, who already passed away in 1929, led the first German military mission. In Germany, Bauer wasn't particularly well adjusted in military high society. His successor, Captain Kriegel, a rude Nazi, was a failure and consequently had to leave. The German government was not much interested in the mission until 1930, when it all changed. A certain general Wetzel was appointed as Chiang Kaj-sjeks top military advisor. In 1934 Wetzel made room for a very prominent figure, general Von Seeckt, who had been Minister of the *Reichswehr* (armed forces) between 1930 and 1932. Von Seeckt, who left again in 1934, put, in that short period, his marks on the Chinese civil war. He defeated

The Japanese expansion in China involved cruelties unheard-of. This picture shows how Chinese prisoners are used during bayonet practice.

the communist army that was fighting the Kuomintang in Southern China, by surrounding their territory with a ring of log cabins that was tightened all the time. The exremely heavy loss suffered by the red army during their escape was followed by their famous 'Long March'.

It was quite damaging for the German-Japanese relations, that the *Aussenamt* and the *Reichswehr*, just shortly after the *Machtsübernahme*, got officially involved in the military mission that was led by general Von Falkenhausen. Since 1934, the delegation came under the Foreign Department of the War Office. That department had a card-index system at its disposal containing all officers serving in China and it was used to select candidates to succeed returning officers. Since 1935 the *HAPRO Handelsgesellschaft* (commercial company) was operational, an idea of the War Office, which was authorised to supply war material to

Chiang Kaj-shek, leader of the Kuomintang, the national people's party.

China and also assisted the construction of their military industry. Both the *Aussenamt* as well as part of the industry supported them in this.

In the meantime the Japanese expansion had continued, at the expense of China. In March 1934 Manchukuo was uplifted to a so-called empire. In those days both Italy and the United States supplied China with advisors and military equipment. In April 1934, the Japanese government announced the Amau declaration. In it, the interference of other nations with the Japanese-Chinese relations was rejected. Selling war material and sending military advisors to China was regarded as a threat to peace. A few days later, the Chinese ambassador in Tokyo was told his country was not allowed to accept any foreign aid without consulting Japan. In addition, in 1935, Japan said goodbye to the existing order in the Pacific region by cancelling the naval convention of Washington and London.

In 1935 and 1936 the Japanese army separated areas southward of Manchukuo from China, in which native collaborators were deployed as administrators. The Kwangtung army provided Inner Mongolia autonomy to utilise it as Pan-Mongolian point of departure for the conquest of the People's Republic of Mongolia. That explains the reason for the alliance between the USSR and the People's Republic of Mongolia that was mentioned earlier.

Even though, between 1931 and 1936, Chiang Kaj-shek called upon assistance – through the League of Nations – from the west, especially American and British, that had little effect. The reason he did not deploy any military resources against Japan during those years originated from his primate of anticommunism. Only when the internal resistance would have been cleared away, it would make sense to take up arms against Japan. Around that same time an internal memo (August 4, 1936) stated that if Japan would invade China any further, armed resistance would follow 'without considering the consequences'. That moment was reached in July 1937. In the meantime a decisive shift had taken place in the politics of China. A rebellious general, the former warlord of Manchuria, Chang Hsueh-liang, took Chiang Kaj-shek prisoner and handed him over to the communists. He was released after negotiations. Result: communism formally placed itself under the authority of the Kuomintang, which boiled down to a united front against Japan.

In June 1937, general Tojo, the chief of staff of the Kwangtung army, sent his superiors a telegram, in which he recommended to attack Kuomintang-China, in order for Japan to have nobody in its back during its imminent confrontation with the USSR. Not all members of Japan's general staff agreed with this plan. A month later a local clash near Peking escalated into an overall Japanese-Chinese war. It started with a clash between Japanese and Chinese troops at the Marco Polo Bridge (Lungchow). When the Japanese Minister of War convinced Prime Minister Konoye to have Japanese troops from Manchukuo and Korea invade Kuomintang territory, it was total war. But Japan kept referring to this conflict by using the understatement 'China incident'. That was apparently a verbal concession to the, in 1928 signed by Japan, Briand-Kellogg Treaty, that committed its participants to settle their disputes in a peaceful manner. China refrained from a declaration of war until December 1941.

In 1937 the combination of the Anti-Comintern Pact and German aid to China became quite difficult. In 1936 the German government had granted a credit of 100 million 'Reichsmark' to China to support the organisation of its military industry. After signing the Anti-Comintern Pact, Minister Blomberg reassured Chiang Kaj-shek with the message that the German-Chinese cooperation would continue as planned. The Japanese authorities depicted their campaign in China as a crusade against communism. From that they drew the conclusion that Germany was violating the Anti-Comintern Pact. The German Secretary of Foreign Affairs, Von Weizsäcker, responded ambassador Mushakoji with the consideration that the actions of Japan strengthened the Chinese communists and drove them into the arms of the USSR. The German Reich received for its arms supplies to China raw materials, like antimony and tungsten, in return; these were essential to the German war economy. When the war had been going on for one month and a half, Hitler told his Minister of Foreign Affairs Von Neurath, that any deliveries based on previous commitments could continue as long as they were covered by currencies or raw materials. *Der Führer* added that any new Chinese orders were not to be accepted, if possible. He said this on the 17th of August 1937. At that moment Germany's commitments of war material deliveries amounted to 223 million *Reichsmark*. After this statement of Hitler new commitments were concluded that amounted to 59 million Mark.

German mediatory efforts to end the war failed early 1938. During that year Japan occupied the complete coast of China, so that the German-Chinese trade was seriously handicapped. In 1938 the *Gleichschaltung* was also completed in Germany. The avowedly pro-Japanese von Ribbentrop succeeded Von Neurath as Minister of Foreign Affairs. The ministerial department of Blomberg was abolished to make room for the *Oberkommando der Wehrmacht* (OKW). Blomberg had protected the military delegation in China with his authority. The mission was now recalled.

In the meantime Italian diplomacy had already taken a pro-Japanese position in 1937. That became clear during the international conference in Brussels. This meeting was called because of an appeal of China to the partners of the Nine-Power Pact, which had confirmed the Open Door policy and sovereignty of China in 1922. Japan that, as we have seen earlier, had tolerated this treaty at that time, did not show up at the conference, but enjoyed the pleasure of the Italian delegation strongly defending Japan's point of view. After Ribbentrop had become Minister of Foreign Affairs, the German Reich finally recognised Manchukuo. In doing so it had been preceded by El Salvador (1934), Italy and Spain. In 1938 it was recognised by Poland as well, subsequently followed by Hungary (1939) and Thailand (1941). The limited number of recognitions underlines the fact that the Stimson-doctrine prevailed.

The 'Pact of Steel'

From 1937 onwards, Ribbentrop aimed at transforming the Anti-Comintern Pact into a military alliance. In October 1937 - so before he became Minister – he claimed the Anti- Comintern Pact was so to speak a wooden bridge, which would make it possible to raise an iron one. As far as that was concerned, it turned out it was possible to have the German and Italian regimes agree, while Japan excluded itself through an imperial veto against joining. Hirohito based this decision on the disagreement about this matter in the Japanese cabinet. The Japanese policy makers, who predominantly came from the army, were fully focused on their expansion in China and also concentrated themselves on an anti-Soviet strategy, in the course of which they wanted to avoid a confrontation with the western nations as much as possible. The expansion lines of Germany and Italy on the other hand, ran in such a way that sooner or later, they would run into Anglo-French resistance. Hitler and Ribbentrop had different opinions relating this matter; the first one hoped on a *modus vivendi* with Great Britain, whereas Ribbentrop believed a German-British conflict could not be avoided. Mussolini agreed with Ribbentrop, because his ambitions in the Mediterranean were focused against Great Britain and France. This difference of opinion between Ribbentrop and Hitler did not create any major obstacles for the latter; the arrogant and stiff diplomat turned out to be very compliant with his leader.

The position Great Britain had taken towards the *Anschluss* and Sudetenland gave the dominant nations of the axis little cause for taking anti-British measures. That changed when the German Reich broke the agreements of Munich in 1939 by forcing the liquidation of the remains of Czechoslovakia. This incident also annoyed Mussolini; he was not consulted and being a former Munich referee, his prestige had suffered. To hold off any further German aggression, the British government subsequently gave guarantees to some of the nations that were possibly threatened by Germany. This was the case for Romania and Greece, but got predominantly significant regarding Poland, whose turn it became not much later, at the next round of German aggression. In April Mussolini compensated oneself for the loss of Italian prestige by occupying Albania. In those days he and Ciano feared that Yugoslavia would disintegrate in such a way that it would lead to the creation of a German satellite state. It was unacceptable for *Il Duce* and his son-in-law to have Germany on the Adriatic. While there was little overlap between Germany's *Drang nach Osten* and Italy's Mediterranean dreams, the lines of expansions threatened to cross one another in Yugoslavia. Ribbentrop however, managed to reassure the Italian leaders on this issue. When his attempts to conclude a German-Japanese-Italian treaty failed because of the one-sided anti-Soviet point of view of Tokyo, he had to be satisfied with a German-Italian alliance. The alliance was signed by the two Ministers of Foreign Affairs, in Berlin on the 22nd of May 1939, in the presence of Hitler. As was laid down in the preamble, both powers were joined by their ideology and the 'solidarity of their interests'. The German and Italian people were also in the future determined to 'act united to safeguard their Lebensraum and maintain peace'. The fact that Lebensraum and peace were not compatible did not really matter, as both regimes were convinced they entered into an alliance for the benefit of a war of aggression. Article I covered the obligation of consultation to come to an agreement in case of common interests or the European situation in general. Article III stipulated that, in case one of the two nations would get involved into a war, the other member of the alliance would take part in the fight with its complete army, 'on land, at sea and in the air'. Article V obligated the allies, in case of a jointly fought war, only to enter into a truce and make peace if its partner is in full agreement.

When this treaty was signed, the Italian government was rightly convinced, that her armed forces were not in great shape. Therefore they verbally claimed – that is to say by way of a statement by Ribbentrop – that Germany would keep the peace for at least three more years. Mussolini and Ciano blamed their German ally very much, that those three years turned out to be three months. Their initial belief in Ribbentrop comes, in the light of the international situation of those days, close to a *credo quia absurdum*. The German demands were after all known and the British government had already issued their guarantees, as was already mentioned. Mussolini could easily have realised, that the German demands on Poland, including its aggression towards that country, threatened to provoke an Anglo-French war against Germany. From the side of the Germans, the obligation of consultation as laid down in the Pact of Steel was not taken very seriously at all. Related to that, the hour of truth was only a few months ahead. On the 21st of August 1939, Ribbentrop gave Ciano a call to inform him that he would be flying to Moscow the next day to sign a political treaty. That sensational blow struck Tokyo even harder; Japan was at war with the USSR and the obligation of consultation Germany had as a result of the Anti-Comintern Pact had been fully neglected.

Japan and the Stalin-Hitler-pact
The fact Japan was only interested in an alliance against the USSR was understandable; while a considerable part of the Japanese armed forces were tied up in China, the armed clashes with the USSR were growing in magnitude. The Red Army turned out to be a fearsome opponent. Both Japan and the USSR were quite discrete about this conflict that hardly received any attention in the West and only found its historian 45 years later, in the person of Alvin Coox. The armed conflicts between Japanese and Russian forces got the characteristics of a local war in the years 1938-1939. In 1937, the Japanese could still fire unpunished at Soviets gunboats on the Amur border river. The Russians reacted weakly to that by leaving some small controversial islands to the Japanese. Furthermore the Soviet officers corps was murderously purged in those days. This resulted in the passing impression within Japanese circles, that the Soviet defence was in disarray. That impression was strengthened when the prominent Soviet

police chief Lyuskov deserted to Japan. That happened in June 1938. The following month the Soviet troops invaded the hilly area of Changkufeng on the border of Manchukuo and Korea. The USSR threw one division after another into battle. Consequently a huge number of bombers, fighters, tanks and heavy artillery were brought into action. The Japanese 19th division was heavily battered. The government in Tokyo —obviously afraid of overextension considering the campaign in China — refused to send reinforcements and bring the air force into action. In August 1938, the Japanese ambassador in Moscow, Shigemitsu and the Soviet People's Commissar of Foreign Affairs, Litvinov worked out a cease-fire. The Japanese troops evacuated the area of dispute. This was seen as a defeat of the Japanese troops in Korea. Within the Kwangtung army the feeling of anger about the defeat spread. It wasn't a surprise that this self-willed force risked a battle against the Red Army. It resulted in a border war that turned out to be much more extensive than the previous one. It started in May 1939 at the border of two satellite states, the People's Republic of Mongolia and Manchukuo. A Japanese cavalry regiment ran into an ambush and most of them were killed. At this location, Japan had come across both Outer Mongolian cavalrymen as well as units of the Red Army. The Kwangtung army forwarded some of its divisions to the scene of action at the border town of Nomonhan. In the beginning of June, Stalin sent for general Zhukov and ordered him to defeat these Japanese troops: 'Tell me what you need and you will get it'. On the 20th of August Zhukov's offensive started, with the result that the Japanese troops had to retreat with heavy losses.

Stalin, who in the case of a war aspired to stay on the

sideline, didn't think France and Great Britain would be reliable allies against Germany. The Conference at Munich had reinforced that belief. But he still kept his options open during the summer of 1939; the USSR was negotiating with France and Great Britain on one side and Germany on the other. Stalin had to consider the possibility of not reaching an agreement with Germany. The countries located between Germany and the USSR made the establishment of an anti-Hitler coalition impossible. Especially Poland would not allow any Soviet troops on its territory in case of war. It showed how much the western Allies respected the fear of Russia's western neighbours for occupation by the Soviets. When Germany gave evidence of willing to pay the price of a tempting Soviet expansion for benevolent Soviet neutrality, the choice of the Kremlin could not be doubtful. Paris and London offered war without an expansion of territory, Germany on the other hand, had peace with an expansion of territory on offer. This resulted on the 22nd of August 1939 in a non-aggression treaty between the USSR and Germany. The secret paragraphs that had been included, provided the USSR during 1939 and 1940 with Eastern Poland (that is to say Western Belo Russia and Northwest Ukraine), the Baltic States as well as Bessarabia. Finland had also come within the sphere of influence of the Soviet Union, but after the Winter War against Finland (November 1939-March 1940) during which the Red Army performed miserably the Soviet government had to content itself with a few peripheral annexations.

The fact that Stalin opted for the pact with Germany was also linked with his actions against Japan. He was very eager to avoid a war on two fronts. At the signing of the treaty Ribbentrop and he exchanged some light remarks on the Anti-Comintern Pact. Stalin said that the treaty in question 'mainly had scared the City of London and the smaller English merchants'. Ribbentrop came with the Berlin joke: 'Stalin will also join the Anti-Comintern Pact'.

Hitler had in common with Stalin, that his motivation for the pact had been strongly determined by Japan. In the case of Germany it evolved around the insufficiency of Japan as an ally. In March 1939, when negotiations were still taking place on a German-Italian alliance with Japan, the Japanese government only wanted to fight a war on the side of its possible treaty partners, when they were attacked by the USSR or another country that in the meantime had become communist (The People's Republic of Mongoloia?). Since Germany and Italy did not border the USSR, whereas Japan had been constantly involved in small and large confrontations with the USSR since 1936, this Japanese reservation formed quite a one-sided and for the two European dictators unacceptable *casus foederis*. The German diplomacy did not consult the Japanese during their negotiations with the USSR, but implied something. After the reception on the occasion of Hitler's birthday (April 20, 1939) Ribbentrop took Oshima and the Japanese ambassador in Rome, Shiratori apart to tell them, that in case Japan would continue to delay an alliance, the German government would feel impelled to contact the Soviets to close a non-aggression treaty. Both diplomats will, without a doubt, have informed their governments about this, who were not at all impressed by it. In Tokyo it was probably regarded as clear bluff. On the 16th of June 1939, Ribbentrop told Shiratori - going a step further –

that it was Germany's intention to close a non-aggression treaty with the USSR. The Polish ambassador in Tokyo had warned Prime Minister Arita already a few days earlier that this was on the way. Shortly afterwards the British ambassador had the same message. Because of this, Arita ordered Oshima to investigate the German relations with the USSR. The ambassador delegated that delicate assignment to one of his assistants, Usami. He paid a visit to Under Secretary Woermann who sent him off none the wiser; the discussions with the USSR had only covered economic matters.

It wasn't until August 21, late in the evening, that Ribbentrop gave Oshima a call – as well as Ciano as we have seen earlier – to inform him he would be flying to Moscow the next day to sign *the* treaty. Oshima immediately answered that this was a flagrant violation of the Anti-Comintern Pact giving evidence of bad faith. The influential daily newspaper *Asahi Shimbun* commented: 'Germany's pact with the archenemy of the Anti-Comintern Pact reduces it to a scrap of paper'. Germany had violated the public part of the Anti-Comintern Pact in spirit, the secret protocol in letter as well. After all it was laid down that consultation would take place regarding the USSR. In addition it said that no treaty would be closed with that country if it affected the interests of the other partner.

On behalf of his government Oshima handed Assistant Secretary von Weiszäcker a clear letter of protest. On recommendation of the Assistant Secretary the disconcerted ambassador took the letter back with him, but nevertheless telegraphed his Prime Minister that he had accomplished the mission. A few months earlier, Oshima had already withheld a very discouraging draft bill concerning the failed triple alliance, because he was afraid to show up with it in Berlin. Obviously, the Japanese establishment wasn't able to keep its self-willed diplomats under control. The Pact meant an enormous loss of face for the Japanese government. For that reason the cabinet of Arita resigned on the 28th of August. Under the next Prime Minister, Abe, not one of the administrators from the previous cabinet returned. In October 1939 Oshima was fired.

Italy: from non-belligerence towards intervention

Among the great powers, Italy was the country with by far the weakest economic and military potential. Nevertheless, in his speeches Mussolini had flaunted with the so-called strength of his country. However, it didn't keep him from complaining in private about the lacking military virtues of the Italian people. While the international crisis around Poland intensified, the question of Italy's obligation as an ally came up. According to the 'pact of steel' the country was obliged to fight on the side of the Germans in case of a possible war. The Italian potential was however so modest, that participation in a European war couldn't be justified. The Italian ambassador in Berlin at that time, Attolico – certainly not a friend of the Nazi's –, came with the idea to transform necessity into virtue; Italy would be willing to go into war on the side of Germany, on the condition that Germany would supply a lot of raw materials on short notice. Mussolini, who rather would have put the *casus foederis* into motion, agreed with Attolico's condition. The Italian shopping list demanded such short time deliveries, that they could never be met. An exasperated Hitler responded: 'The Italians do the same as in 1914'. (At that time Italy remained neutral, in spite of its *Dreibund* with Germany and Austria-Hungary, before it joined the allies in 1915.) Ciano referred to Ribbentrop's prognoses, that it might take another three years before war would break out. This non-belligerence by necessity of the country distressed *Il Duce*, who was very sensitive to prestige. He firmly believed that Italy could only become a great nation through war. It was one of his ambition's to replace Britain maritime supremacy in the Mediterranean by Italian dominance, while he was eager to have France dispose of Nice, Savoy, Corsica and Tunesia. As the Germans attacked Poland, he asked Hitler for a statement in which the ally Italy was absolved for its non-belligerence. According to that request, Hitler had to thank him for Italy's diplomatic support and declare that Germany, relying on its own strength, didn't require any Italian assistance. *Der Führer* actually did send a message that corresponded with Mussolini's wishes. The Italian press brought the news extensively, while the Germans were silent as the grave. Subsequently, the German-Italian relations were quite tense until February 1940. Furthermore a persistent difference of opinion arose between Mussolini and Ciano. Mussolini wanted, at the right moment, to join Germany in its war. Ciano, who did not believe in a German victory, aimed at lasting neutrality. The first months it hardly gave any complications since *Il Duce* and his son-in-law shared the same irritations regarding Germany at that time. A typical example of that is their negative approach to the rapprochement between Germany and the USSR. Mussolini, for example let out accidentally: 'Hitler will regret it some day, that he opened the door to Europe for the Russians'. But still the Italian regime didn't dare to turn its back on the German switch towards Moscow. They even showed an understanding for it. Ciano wrote in his diary on October 16, 1939: 'He (Mussolini) wants to start a campaign to make it clear to the Italians that Bolshevism is dead and has been replaced by a Soviet fascism'. That would actually mean there was no longer a basis for the Anti-Comintern Pact. Ciano apparently did not share Mussolini's view on 'Soviet fascism', for he characterised the Stalin-Hitler pact as a 'regression into barbarism'. 'It is our historical duty to put up a fight against this with every weapon and means'. He added however, that he doubted the possibility of that 'historical' assignment, because of the decisions that had already been made.

The leading duo cultivated moral indignation, especially regarding the German excesses in Poland and expressed their willingness to cause the German Reich some inconvenience. So they maintained their own diplomatic delegation in Warsaw during the autumn of 1939 and also still recognised Poland's government in exile. An Italian report on the German misbehaviour in Posen (Poznan) made Mussolini so furious, that he asked Ciano to pass this information on to the American and British press. When Ciano wrote this in his diary on the 4th of December, the USSR had started its unglorious campaign against Finland a couple of days earlier. Ciano promised the Finnish attaché supplies and opened his own office for aid to Finland. That was in heavy contrast with Germany that observed a well-disposed aloofness towards the USSR concerning the Winter War. In Italy fierce student demonstrations were allowed, against the USSR and in favour of Finland. In relation to this, Ciano also wrote in his diary on the 4th of December: 'We should not forget, that people by saying "death to Russia" actually mean "death to Germany". That obviously pleased him.

Simultaneously Ciano obstructed Germany in Japan as well. Through the Italian ambassador in Tokyo, Auriti, Ciano sabotaged the German attempts to accomplish closer relations between Japan and the USSR. Ciano also gave instructions to promote anti-German tendencies in the Japanese press. It was the Italian administrator's recommendation, to encourage the anti-Russian position as well as the advances towards the United States of America. The German ambassador in Tokyo, Ott (the former military attaché, who had succeeded Von Dirksen in 1937), found out and discussed it with his Italian colleague. He pointed out the pro-allied nature of the Italian interferences. Subsequently the German ambassador in Rome complained to Ciano about Auriti's behaviour. Consequence: Auriti was acquitted of his responsibilities, while he had only carried out Ciano's instructions.

Mussolini's anti-German contestations were primarily based on *jalousie de métier*. There was nothing he feared more than a German triumph in which Italy had no part. Because he simply could not go to war in 1939, he preferred a peace based on compromise, which would allow him to gain prestige again in his role as an arbitrator. It was for this reason he appealed to Hitler with the unfeasible proposition to recreate a small Poland. Mussolini did this in a letter dated January 5, 1940, in which he also warned against close relations with the USSR. He pointed out that the German-Russian pact in Spain had made a painful impression that benefited the Allies. He also paid attention to the German complaints about the trade policy of the Italians. The export to France and Great Britain was aimed at providing Italy with the necessary currency to import raw materials, which were necessary to strengthen its armament. He admitted the relationship of Italy with the USSR was poor, 'but he would do nothing to make it worse, in spite of his sympathy for the brave people of Finland'. A smaller Poland ought to be created, only inhabited by Poles. That would be sufficient as a condition for peace, since Germany did not strive for any objectives of war in the West. He argued that it would be impossible for France and Great Britain to conquer Germany, but also was in doubt whether Germany would be able to defeat an Anglo-French coalition that was supported by the United States. 'In the end there would only be vanquished'. He implored Hitler not to give up his anti-bolshevist identity and 'that intensifying your relationship with Moscow would have catastrophic consequences in Italy'. The German Living Space was in Russia and it was Germany's task to defend Europe against Asia. Mussolini was trying to play *Mein Kampf* off against the current German strategy.

Within the German establishment there were actually potential dissidents who agreed with Mussolini's letter. That applied especially to the German ambassador in Rome, Von Hassell, the chief of the *Abwehr*, admiral Canaris and Assistant Secretary Von Weitzäcker. Five days later, on the 5th of January, Ribbentrop told Attalico that Hitler would 'probably' answer in writing. He added that the real answer would consist of the great German offensive, which would make Mussolini's objections obsolete.

Not receiving an answer from Hitler surely was humiliating, but at the same time Mussolini showed a growing aversion against the British Empire. Within the framework of their strategy of blockades, the British set up an embargo against the German export of coal to Italy, that took place through Rotterdam and Antwerp. In compensation they were willing to deliver their own coal. Ciano wanted to accept that, Mussolini's didn't. *Il Duce* experienced the maritime predominance of Great Britain, especially in the Adriatic, as an unacceptable humiliation that supplied him with additional motivation to direct him towards joining the German warfare.

On the 10th of March 1940, Ribbentrop arrived in Rome. He carried the answer of Hitler on Mussolini's letter with him. Hitler argued in his letter, that given the community of destiny *(Schicksalgemeinschaft)* between both nations, it was inevitable that Italy would join the German warfare. Furthermore, he assured Germany would provide Italy with its need for coal (now being transported over land). He also argued that during the war an autonomous Poland was out of the question and showed his understanding for the Russian attitude towards Finland. Ribbentrop clarified the letter in more detail. Regarding the USSR he did that with a forced optimism. Talking about the really remarkable 'de-Jewification' of the Soviet government, he went as far as to doubt whether the prominent Soviet politician Kaganovitch (= son of Cohen!) was Jewish, who according to him had a Georgian appearance. Ribbentrop said about Finland that the Minister of Foreign Affairs, Tanner was a Menshevik who had a bad influence. As a result of British machinations a situation was created which left Russia no other option than to intervene. Ribbentrop and Mussolini agreed that Russia had abandoned the world revolution and had returned to an in essence tsarist regime. (It is striking, that in those days the national-socialist and fascist nomenclature constantly talked about Russia instead of the Soviet Union.) It was agreed that Hitler and Mussolini would meet each other on the 8th of March at the Brenner-pass.

That meeting involved five persons, two dictators, their Ministers of Foreign Affairs and the chief of protocol, P. Schmidt, who acted as interpreter as well. It ended in a monologue of Hitler, almost reducing *Il Duce* to a state of speechlessness. Most of it covered a repetition of what already had been written in Hitler's letter and had been argued in Ribbentrop's last visit to Rome. Hitler emphasized, that if Italy would remain non-belligerent, it would have to be satisfied with a second-class position in the Mediterranean. He claimed that the attitude of the British had left him with no other option than to approach Russia. Mussolini promised once again that Italy would join the German warfare as soon as possible.

That was quite contradictory to what Ciano had told the American Under Secretary, Sumner Welles, the month before: 'Tell him (president Roosevelt) that Italy will not join Germany in war as long as I am Minister of Foreign Affairs. I will do everything within my power to influence Mussolini in that direction.' This last intention wasn't a success. Shortly after the meeting at the Brenner, the Italian press used quite a belligerent tone. Until May of 1940, people in the leading circles of Italy have been sceptical about Hitler's intentions against France, but that became quite different after this.

During the fast German advance in France, Ciano met with the French and British ambassadors to hand them the Italian declaration of war. However, he did not resign! Italy played no part in the collapse of the French resistance. Still Italy, like Spain, claimed French colonial territory in North Africa, which was brushed aside by the Germans. In the shadow of the Third Reich, Italy, unnoticed, signed a separate cease-fire with France. Hitler vetoed the Italian claims on territory in North Africa, because he feared that France would then put its fleet at the disposal of the British and would continue the fight from Africa. That consideration played a major part in the meeting Hitler and Mussolini had in Munich on the 18th of June, a few days before the two cease-fires with France.

The realisation of the Tripartite Pact

On the 15th of September 1939, Japan and the USSR agreed to a cease-fire. The chilling of the Japanese relations with Germany did not cause an approach towards the West. The proclamation of Japan's 'New Order' in Eastern Asia remained unacceptable for the United States, Great Britain and France. In July 1939, the United States announced that the trade treaty with Japan would be terminated early 1940, which implied restrictions, but not an embargo.

In March 1940, the Japanese government installed a satellite regime in Nanking under the leadership of Wang Ching-wei, a former Kuomintang rival of Chiang Kaj-shek. The American Secretary of State, Cordell Hull, heavily condemned this. He emphasised that the Kuomintang regime that had fled to Chungking, was the only legitimate government of China. In addition, the United States increased their support to China.

Since 1938 Japan controlled the coast of China, which hindered, but did not completely cut off the import of weapons. The aid from the USSR by means of sending material, advisors and pilots continued. Some foreign commerce was preserved through British Burma and French Indochina.

The German subjection of The Netherlands and

The Russian minister Molotov (left) as a tough negotiator. Next to him Frick and a translator. On the right von Ribbentrop and a smoking Reichsführer-SS Himmler.

France (May-June 1940) caused a major shift in favour of Japan and at the expense of China. The British, in the critical situation they were in, felt impelled to temporarily close the Burma-road. Of a more lasting significance to the further development of the war was the fact that the French collaboration regime had to admit Japanese troops into Northern Indochina. This resulted in a further deterioration of the Japanese-American relations. The Japanese tried to obtain economic privileges in the Dutch East Indies, but the negotiations in question failed. Besides, the colonial Netherlands was hoping on support from the United States. Already in April 1940, a few weeks before the German occupation of The Netherlands, Washington warned Tokyo against violating the status quo in the Dutch East Indies. Directing the American Pacific fleet from San Diego to Hawaii reinforced this.

In the summer of 1940 it became evident, that the pro-allied non-belligerence of the United States was a serious obstacle for both Germany and Japan; the persistent British and Chinese belligerence against the New Order was based on heavy support from the United States. That's why Germany, Italy and Japan shaped an alliance mainly based on mutual anti-American interests. The most important objective of the Tripartite Pact, which was concluded by them in September 1940, was to prevent the United States from waging war against the New Order. This was stated in article 3 of the pact. After they had acknowledged the leadership of each other in the New Order of Europe and 'Great-East-Asia' in article 1 and 2, they came, in article 3, with the promise 'to help each other with all political, economic and military means, in case one of the partners is attacked by a nation who is not yet involved in the European war and the Chinese-Japanese conflict'. The fact they spoke of a Chinese–Japanese conflict instead of war was the result of using Japanese nomenclature. The Japanese authorities specified their belligerence as the 'China-incident'. This was a tribute to the Briand-Kellogg-pact (1928), which had been signed by Japan and codified the peaceful settlement of international conflicts.

The prelude to the pact mainly took place in Tokyo. It's there that Ribbentrop's confidant Stahmer, assisted by ambassador Ott, negotiated with the Japanese Minister of Foreign Affairs, Matsuoka. They were under time pressure, because the Nazi regime – Ribbentrop in front – was in a hurry, which was based on motives of prestige and propaganda. On the part of the Japanese it was laid down in a secret paragraph that the execution of article 3 would be subject to consultation between the three treaty partners. Stahmer had agreed to it and promised to inform Ribbentrop upon his return home, which he failed to do. After the war, the allied researchers didn't find that exchange of letters in the files of the *Aussenamt*.

It meant that Japan remained a questionable ally. In the negotiations that took place later on and failed, the Japanese diplomacy repeatedly implied that Japan would, without terminating it, not use the Tripartite Pact against the United States, if Washington would be willing to spare the New Order in Eastern-Asia. Berlin expected something like that. This is why the allied relationship remained suspicious in between the autumns of 1940 and 1941. On the 10th of June 1941, the German Naval Attaché in Tokyo, admiral Wenneker informed his superiors based on information from the Japanese navy, that the Japanese authorities, in case of extension of the war, would only observe the *casus foederis* if it would suit them well.

The fact that the preliminary stage of the Tripartite Pact was an almost exclusively Japanese-German affair was a consequence of the insignificant war performance of Italy. The once so boastful and ostentatious regime of Mussolini got, in comparison with the impressive performance of the Third Reich, more and more into a secondary position. But the treaty had the complete approval of Mussolini. The signing of the treaty, which took place in Berlin, was a pompously staged event.

Article 5 gave a reassuring message to the Kremlin: 'Germany, Italy and Japan confirm that the conditions mentioned earlier, in no way will affect the political situation that exists between each of the three treaty partners and the Soviet Union.' It goes without saying that this was not enough to reassure the, at all times, suspicious Soviet government. The *Pravda* took cognisance of it with satisfaction, but also observed, that the paragraph on 'each of the three treaty partners' did not interfere with their consensus concerning the Anti-Comintern Pact.

The USSR played an important role in the negotiations that preceded the Tripartite Pact. Since the surrender of France and The Netherlands opened new perspectives for the Japanese expansion in South-East Asia, it was very important for Tokyo to secure the peace with Russia in the north. It is for that reason that Ribbentrop and Stahmer promised the Japanese government that German diplomacy would gladly contribute to an improvement of Japanese-Russian relations. That is quite remarkable, since Hitler had already decided on his aggression towards the USSR in July 1940. It looks as if Ribbentrop wasn't aware of Hitler's intentions regarding this in the autumn of 1940…

The extension of the Tripartite Pact

The collapse of France persuaded Stalin into rapidly getting hold of the catch that, as a result of the secret paragraphs of the non-aggression treaty with Germany, lied ahead of him. As a result, the three Baltic countries were energetically annexed, while Romania was impelled to give up Bessarabia and North-Bukovina. This last territory wasn't covered by the secret paragraphs. At the moment that Molotov informed German ambassador Von der Schulenberg, of this intention, they still demanded the annexation of the whole of Bukovina. The German objection against this demand, led to a situation in which the ultimatum of the Soviets to Romania remained limited to North-Bukovina. In the absence of German support, the Romanian government gave in to the Soviet demands and subsequently pressed itself fearfully against the Third Reich; a fact that would become convenient to Hitler in preparation of his war against the USSR.

The USSR had now gotten hold of everything the secret paragraphs promised, with the exception of Finland. This exception was a consequence of the Winter War. The Red Army had made a bad impression there, after which Stalin contented himself with a few annexations during the Peace of Moscow, in March 1940. Some additional Soviet demands followed in June 1940. The most important one referred to the nickel mines of Petsamo, which the USSR wanted to take over in commission. Hitler considered these mines to be of vital importance for German warfare. That's why the German government concluded a treaty with Finland in July 1940, in which was stated that 60 % of the Finnish production of nickel would go to Germany. With this a German-Russian matter of dispute was forshadowed.

Although the German Reich had done nothing to support Finland during the Winter War, the Finnish government cherished the hope to re-conquer the lost territory some day in the future with the help from Germany and to possibly add the East-Karelian territory to it, which already belonged to the USSR before 1939. In July 1940 Hitler decided to attack the USSR. A month later Germany started to supply Finland with weapons again. Additional German troops gathered in North-Norway during those days, in order to prevent a possible Soviet attack on the nickel mines. In return for the weapon supplies, the Finnish government was also willing to grant the

German troops passage on their way to North-Norway. Already in September 1940, the commander of the German mountain troops in North-Norway, general Dietl, drew up a German-Finnish plan of operations against the USSR, named *Unternehmen Renntier* (Operation Reindeer). At that time Finland wasn't aware yet — as many other countries — of the German plans of attack against the USSR. Furthermore Finland tried to distance oneself from the New Order. Unlike Germany's other allies, it never joined the Tripartite Pact.

Romania on the other hand, got a new regime in 1940 that eagerly subordinated itself to the New Order. It didn't look like that in 1939. After the German elimination of Czechoslovakia it received, like Poland, a French-British guarantee. Having become timid after the split up of Poland between Germany and the USSR, the Romanian government asked the British whether the guarantee also applied to possible Soviet aggression, but came away empty handed. After France was brought down, German protection was all that remained for the Romanian government. Enemies surrounded the country. After abandoning territory to the USSR, also Hungary and Bulgaria presented their territorial claims. The fact that Germany and Italy recommended the Romanian authorities in June 1940 to give way to the Soviet ultimatum, was mainly founded on the fear of a Russian-Romanian war that would endanger the export of petroleum to the Axis-powers. Subsequently Ribbentrop and Ciano mediated in the Hungarian and Bulgarian claims of territory on Romania. By virtue of the second *Wiener Schiedspruch* (the first Vienna Arbitration in 1938 concerned the Hungarian and Polish territory claims on Czechoslovakia) Romania had to give up

Northern Transylvania to Hungary. That meant the loss of a territory with 2.5 million inhabitants, including 1 million Romanians. The loss of South-Dobrudzha to Bulgaria on the other hand wasn't unbearable. What was left of Romania received a German-Italian guarantee, something the USSR of course considered as an unfriendly act. Although the USSR supported the Hungarian and Bulgarian territorial claims, the Soviet government protested in Berlin about the *Schiedspruch* since this fait accompli was a violation of article 3 of the German-Russian non-aggression treaty, which mentioned the duty of consultation on matters that affected both countries. At this protest they also demanded the annexation of South-Bukovina, as well as the annulment of the denounced German-Italian guarantee. On the 21st of September, the USSR suddenly occupied a number of islands in the northern arm of the Danube, called the Kilia, as a result of which Romania was deprived of a considerable part of the delta.

After these humiliating losses of territory, king Carol had to leave. The words of his son and successor Michael did not carry any weight against general Antonescu, who established a dictatorial regime. He requested to send a German military mission; Hitler agreed to this on the 11th of September 1940, which was 10 days after the Soviet usurpation in the Kilia. Soon it involved a lot more than a mission; in November 1940 there were already 23 thousand German soldiers, while Romania, towards the spring of 1941, granted passage to the German troops that invaded Greece through Bulgaria.

The situation on the Balkans became even more complicated when Italian forces invaded Greece, ergo Epirus, from Albania in the night of the 27th and 28th of October

1940. As mentioned before, a few weeks earlier Germany had stationed troops in Romania to protect the supply of petroleum. Now also *Il Duce*, who again hadn't been consulted, was faced with an accomplished fact that he tried to compensate with a military adventure. On October 12, 1940 Mussolini said, as a result of the German actions in Romania: 'Every time Hitler faces me with a fait accompli. This time I will pay him back in his own coin. He will read in the newspaper that I have occupied Greece. This way balance will return.' Even his sceptical son-in-law, who wrote this down in his diary, added: 'I also really believe that the military operation will run smoothly and will be of great benefit to us.' It turned out to be a fatal miscalculation. A major part of Albania was conquered by the Greeks, as a result of which Germany had to compensate the Italian weakness in the Balkans, which meant that the campaign against the USSR began six weeks later than was originally planned.

The encampment of German troops in Romania displeased the USSR obviously even more than Italy, whereas in Finland, Germany impinged on the sphere of influence it had assigned the USSR in 1939. When we also remember that Hitler had already decided in July 1940 to wage war against the USSR, it is remarkable that Molotov paid his respects in Berlin in November to negotiate about the Soviets joining the Tripartite Pact. It speaks for itself there was no chance of a Quadripartite Pact. Hitler was thinking of the idea, apparently inspired by Ribbentrop, of a Eurasian bloc that would extend from Japan to Spain. With that, Great Britain would be isolated and the inviolability of the New Order would be underlined. Accordingly it was suggested to Molotov that the war against Great Britain had already been won. The Soviet top diplomat, who made an uncommunicative and cunning impression to the Nazi's, reacted with ironical scepticism. Hitler hoped to link the USSR temporarily with the New Order, among other things to redirect the expansion lines of the Soviets towards South Asia. Molotov thought that was interesting, but wasn't distracted. On the contrary, he became so concrete on the subject of Europe, that he strengthened Hitler in his intention to wage war against the USSR. The demands Molotov put forward were quite suitable to help Germany in acquiring allies.

The demands of the Soviets boiled down to the following items:

1. Annexation of Finland;
2. Annulment of the German-Italian guarantee to Romania and annexation of South- Bukovina;
3. Soviet guarantee to Bulgaria, which would bring that country within Moscow's sphere of influence;
4. Soviet naval bases on the Dardanelles.

The first and second demands were of course very advantageous for the bond of Finland and Romania to the New Order.

On November 26, Molotov informed ambassador Von der Schulenburg that the USSR was willing to extend the Tripartite Pact to a Quadruple Pact by joining in case the four above-mentioned demands were met. He added as a fifth demand that Japan would give up South-Sakhalin to the USSR. Hitler's reaction was so negative that he did not allow Ribbentrop to answer to the proposal of the Soviets.

Hitler's negotiations with Molotov had been in so far serious, that he surely aspired to isolate Great Britain. In addition, the argued expansion of the Soviets in the direction of South-Asia would have been quite suitable to have the Soviets collide with the British. That would have given him an ideal point of departure for the coming war against the USSR.

Romania joined the Tripartite Pact on the 23rd of November. Hungary, like Germany, needed a revision of the peace decrees that had followed upon the First World War. Those irredentist claims of revision were partly realised in the trail of the New Order. In November 1938 a strip of South-Slovakia was annexed, which was followed, in March 1939, by the annexation of Ruthenia (Carpathian-Ukraine). Accordingly Hungary joined the Anti-Comintern Pact in February 1939 – together with Manchukuo – and left the League of Nations in April 1939. In the spring of 1938 anti-Semitic laws were introduced, which were extended in May 1939. Hungary joined the Tripartite Pact on November the 20th, an example that was followed by Slovakia three days later. Partly as a result of Molotov's exacting attitude, the European part of the Tripartite Pact got a definite anti Soviet tendency. This didn't apply to Bulgaria, which didn't join the Pact until the 1st of March 1941. By the way, in the spring of 1941, Bulgaria had become of vital importance to Germany, because of the escalation of the war in the Balkans.

Mainly two aspects determined this escalation, the weakness of Italy opposite Greece and the pro-allied tendencies in Yugoslavia. Under heavy pressure of Germany, Yugoslavia joined the Tripartite Pact on the 25th of March. Two days later the prince regent Paul was overthrown by way of a coup, which brought a certain general Simovich in power, after which his government annulled the Tripartite Pact. Although Simovich claimed he would remain neutral, Hitler decided to invade Yugoslavia and take Greece along as well. Yugoslavia, vulnerable from an inter-ethnical point of view, disintegrated quickly, while Greece was crushed during the course of April. Yugoslavia was now split up in the following way: Germany divided Slovenia with Italy, that annexed the Dalmatian coast, added Kosovo to its dependency Albania and was allowed to appoint the monarch of the new small satellite Montenegro from its own dynasty, while Croatia became a separate fascist state, Vojvodina in the east was handed over to Hungary, Serbia was placed under military rule and Bulgaria nestled in Macedonia. The German Balkan campaign meant that the attack of the USSR had to be postponed with six weeks. A delay of which Hitler claimed in 1945 that it had been fatal to him.

In preparation of the campaign against the USSR, Operation Barbarossa, it was of major importance to Hitler, that Romania and Finland put their territory at his disposal. The fact they also joined him in order to reclaim lost territory, was convenient to him. He still didn't have a coalition war in mind. Initially he considered the campaign against the USSR to be an exclusively German assignment.

Concerning Japan there was a communication failure once again. In March 1941, Minister Matsuoka travelled to Europe without any clear instructions. Through a lack of consensus within the Japanese government no directives had been drafted. Policies became even more complicated because of the character of the government official that had been sent abroad. He was a spirited, somewhat unstable person with extreme ideas that could suddenly change drastically. Although he had heard that the German-Russian relations were not that good anymore, he stated to

Stalin in Moscow, on his way to Berlin, that Japan, Germany and the USSR had a common interest in reducing the Anglo-American power. Apparently he held on to Ribbentrop's outdated concept of a Japanese-German deal with the USSR, which would intimidate the British and Americans. Hitler and Ribbentrop told him nevertheless that the German-Russian relations were deteriorating quickly, although he wasn't brought up to date on the coming aggression against the USSR. Of course Matsuoka couldn't convert the German leaders to his Quadruple concept. In turn they could not get his promise that Japan would attack the British Empire in South-Asia on short notice. He also wasn't authorised to make such a promise. On the way back, Matsuoka visited Moscow once again, where he signed a neutrality pact with the USSR. It underlines again, that Japan and Germany never succeeded in coordinating their policy towards the USSR. In the treaty Japan and the USSR recognised the territorial integrity of their respective satellite states, Manchukuo and the People's Republic of Mongolia.

On the 2nd of June 1941 *Der Führer* and *Il Duce* met again at the Brenner. Hitler declared that it was difficult for him to understand Matsuoka. He had put all his hopes on Oshima who had returned as ambassador to Berlin in March 1941. Again nothing was mentioned about the coming German belligerence against the USSR. The only two nations that received any advance knowledge – late and incomplete nonetheless - on Operation Barbarossa were Finland and Romania, obviously because of their indispensability.

Between Barbarossa and Pearl Harbor

The fact that Hitler was little forthcoming towards his allies during his preparation of operation Barbarossa had to do with discretion. In that respect he was particularly suspicious towards the leading circles in Italy and Hungary. That's why these two nations were kept in the dark as long as possible. Even on the 2nd of June Ribbentrop declared to Ciano that any rumours about a German operation against the USSR were 'unfounded and at least premature'. This was also the way it was played with Hungary. When Horthy visited the *Führerhauptquartier* on the 24th of April 1941, Hitler told him the relations between Germany and the USSR were *'völlig korrekt'*. Although the Romanian dictator Antonescu, being Hitler's ally against the USSR, was very motivated, during the spring of 1941 the German military mission had to maintain the idea towards the military authorities that the German concentrations of troops had a defensive purpose. Germany also had its reasons to be worried about the internal stability of Romania. That was especially valid for the Iron Guard, a movement that had a lot in common with the Nazi's. In 1940 Antonescu incorporated the Guard in his proclaimed regime, but this resulted in chaos. The slaughters of the Guard among Jews, including looting and arson, as well as murders of hostile scientists, drove even the Nazi's mad. Martin Ros mentioned in his essay on the Iron Guard, that Hitler had 'no interest in an outburst of radical Romanian-fascist nationalism'. That's why German soldiers assisted Antonescu during his oppression of the Iron Guard in February 1941. Leaders of the Guard, including their leader Horia Sima, were put in German concentration camps. There they were, according to Ros on Himmler's instructions, 'kept in a reasonable condition'. When later on, in August 1944, the Antonescu regime was brought down Sima and his group were to be used as collaborators again.

Not until the 12th of June 1941, during a meeting with Antonescu in Munich, Hitler informed the Romanian leader of the coming operation. Even now Hitler persisted in a supposedly defensive concept. He claimed that the Russian concentrations of troops made a preventive war necessary. There wasn't a question of common planning or objectives. The German military mission wasn't too impressed with the Romanian armed forces, which were put into action with full belief by Antonescu. On June 20 he gave his general staff the necessary directives for operation 'Munich', i.e. the advance of Romanian troops across the Pruth to re-conquer Bessarabia. Hitler entrusted Antonescu with the formal high command of the German and Romanian troops in Romania. Whereas the Romanian regime, if it had gotten the chance, would have felt for a coalition war, the Finnish government tried to keep its warfare away from the New Order as much as possible. Soon after the Winter War, the Finnish government under the leadership of Ryti hoped for a deterioration of the German-Russian relations, which would enable the country to re-conquer its lost territories.

Although the German military planning expected already in the autumn of 1940 that Finland would participate in the coming campaign, the Finnish authorities were not informed until May 20, 1941. This happened by way of a mission of envoy Schnurre. He also told them about the demands concerning Finland that Molotov had put forward. Within that context, a Finnish military mission was invited. During the negotiations that followed, it turned out that the Finnish generals were not inclined to take part in the, by the Germans, planned encirclement of Leningrad. Hitler did stipulate that Finland postponed the mobilisation until the start of operation Barbarossa, as he did not want to provoke any preventive measures from the side of the Soviets. When the war had commenced, it is true that Finland mobilised, but the government also made a statement of neutrality. That was incompatible with the German declaration of war that was launched the same day. It said, that German soldiers, together with Finnish divisions, were located on the Arctic and in Finland 'in order to jointly protect the country'. Based on constitutional grounds, Finland wanted to leave the first acts of war to the USSR. After fire had been opened from the Soviet base Hanko and Soviet fighters bombed Finnish ships, after which bombardments followed on Helsinki and Turku, the Finnish government had collected enough supporting evidence on the 26th of June to issue a declaration of war.

The Japanese government, which was badly informed, also because of the hardly receptive attitude of Matsuoka, was again hit quite unpleasantly. Just like at the Stalin-Hitler-pact, Germany had flagrantly violated her obligations of consultation. The Japanese government had still held on to the outdated Ribbentrop-concept of an USSR that was associated with the New Order and would be kept away from the allied camp as a result of its benevolent neutrality. Now that this prospect had collapsed, Prime Minister Konoye understood that the USSR would look for Anglo-American support and as a result had ended up in the camp of the western Allies. He feared that Japan would end up being at war with all those countries; a fear that became a reality in the final stage of the Second World War. Now the question came up, what to do next? Konoye was of opinion that the pact with the Axis-powers was no longer useful, probably even harmful. That's why he thought Japan had to tear itself away from Germany to aim at a deal with the United States. Early July 1941 he wrote Matsuoka that Japan could not afford a war with both the United States and the USSR. These two nations should not be driven into each other's arms. The most critical topic was the fact that, regarding its supply of raw materials, especially petroleum, Japan was dependent on the United States and, to a lesser extent, on the Dutch East Indies. It meant that Japanese concessions concerning China and Southeast-Asia would be difficult to avoid. That's why Konoye's attempt to come to a diplomatic deal with the United States wasn't feasible. His view differed from Matsuoka's. Immediately after the German attack on the USSR this foreign minister proposed in vain to declare war against the USSR. Shortly afterwards he was discharged, which was also linked with his anti-American attitude.

On the 6th of September 1941, in the presence of the emperor, the decision was made that Japan had to be at full war-strength in October and if there was no deal with the United States at that time, had to venture the leap southward. That would mean war with the so-called *ABCD*-nations (*A*merica, Great *B*ritain, *C*hina and The Netherlands in this case the *D*utch East-Indies).

The Italian reaction to operation Barbarossa was, as far as Mussolini is concerned, quite remarkable. The German fait accompli was presented the following way. On the 22nd of June at three o'clock in the morning, the German ambassador handed Ciano a letter of Hitler for Mussolini.

At that time Mussolini was at home, where the message of war from the letter reached him by telephone. He then told his wife spontaneously: 'My dear Rachele, that means the war has been lost.' In spite of this defeatist statement, he became a supporter of Italian participation in the war against the USSR for prestigious considerations.

Germany's smaller allies formed a heterogeneous group, which looked at Operation Barbarossa in various ways. Although the Horthy-regime was very anticommunist, Hitler didn't allow the Hungarian authorities to be informed about his plan of war before the middle of June. Still the Hungarian ambassador in Berlin, Sztojay, who got wind of the coming campaign a little earlier, urged his Prime Minister, Bardossy, on June the 2nd, to offer the German authorities as soon as possible Hungarian participation in a possible war against the USSR. It would make a good impression in Berlin and in his opinion victory was beyond all doubt. On the 15th of June Ribbentrop informed Bardossy in confidence of what was ahead. On the 22nd of June Horthy received a similar letter from Hitler and being 'an old crusader against Bolshevism' he reacted with great enthusiasm. Nevertheless the Hungarian government did not go any further on the 23rd of June than breaking the relations with the USSR. War wasn't declared until June 26, as a result of a dubious Soviet air raid. The cause of it lied in the anticommunist principles and poisonous rivalry with Romania. Hungary had gone through a communist regime in 1919, which was followed by the reaction of an authoritarian, fiercely anticommunist regime. The other motive laid in the problem of nationalities; if Hungary did not take part in the war, it would, with the expected German victory in mind, be worse off compared with

Slovakia and especially Romania, which both housed an Hungarian minority. In order to prevent Romanians, Slovaks and Croats – who all fought the USSR – to intrigue against Hungary in Berlin, Hungary would have to perform successfully in the war against the USSR, according to Sztojay. Considering Finland, Romania, Croatia, Slovakia and Hungary, while adding various groups of volunteers, the attack on the USSR appeared to be a crusade against Bolshevism. That didn't prevent Hitler and his aides from determining the operational policy on their own. Concerning Hungary, the German Reich especially benefited from the Peace of Trianon (1920), under which Hungary became so mutilated, that it tried to re-conquer its territory by way of the New Order. The Romanian regime, in turn, hoped to make such a good impression in the war, that the Hungarian annexation of Northern Transylvania would be annulled with German approval. Hitler had already given Antonescu hope regarding this matter during their meeting of November 23, 1940. During that occasion the German leader argued that the *Wiener Schiedspruch* wasn't an ideal solution and history would not stop in 1940.

During the first successful months of the war, Romania did not only re-conquer Bessarabia and North-Bukovina, but was also entrusted by the Germans with the administration of the territory between the Dnjestr and the Bug, Transnistria. The Romanians got the administration over Transnistria without annexing it. According to Barbara Jelavich they did not want that because they were afraid that it would then be regarded as a compensation for the loss of Northern Transylvania; that would make the unacceptable second *Wiener Schiedsspruch* irreversible.

Her colleague Hitchins is of opinion that Hitler had made this a condition. He would only allow Romania to annex Transnistria, if the country renounced its claim upon Northern Transylvania.

One of the disadvantages of the satellite status to which Hungary and Romania were reduced, was that German minorities were to be privileged in such a way that they became so to speak a state within a state. Additionally Germany placed high demands on the Romanian economy, especially concerning petroleum and grain. The high losses on the front and the economic hardships weakened Antonescu's regime towards the winter and led to internal tensions. The Hungarian war efforts were a lot less than the Romanian. It applied, as a remainder of sovereignty, that the Hungarian as well as Romanian regime – both were exclusively anti-Soviet – avoided a situation of war with the western Allies until the end of 1941.

Finland became more and more dependent on Germany, but managed to avoid the status of a satellite. During the entire war, Jewish soldiers and officers remained in the Finnish army. The warfare was being presented as the defence of Europe against the East, but as a matter of fact was being spared genocide and ideological balderdash. The Finnish government saw it necessary to join the Anti-Comintern Pact, which had been put back to life as a result of Operation Barbarossa, in the autumn of 1941. Joining was inevitable as Finland was dependent on the Third Reich for its food supply. During the winter of 1941, Finland's ideological concession was honoured with the supply of 750 thousand ton's of grain. Finland remained outside the Tripartite Pact. Within the Anti-Comintern Pact, Finland got company from Denmark, where the social-democratic government joined in November 1941, under extreme pressure from Ribbentrop.

In November 1941, the Anti-Comintern Pact, which had been drafted for a five-year period, was up for renewal. For this reason the member states held a conference in Berlin that was chaired by Ribbentrop. The public part of the treaty was renewed by all member states, but Japan cancelled the secret paragraph in order not to endanger its neutrality towards the USSR. In his biography of Ribbentrop, Bloch points out that he could not say much in his speech about the shaping of the New Order in Europe; the censorship of Hitler, who didn't want to establish any images of the future, played its part. Seven new member states were welcomed. China (the collaboration government of Wang Ching-wei), Croatia, Slovakia, Romania, Bulgaria, as well as the earlier mentioned Finland and Denmark, who in fact did not belong to the New Order.

Although Mussolini's reaction to the news of operation Barbarossa had been defeatist, he was soon willing, for reasons of prestige, to send an Italian army corps to the eastern front. In October 1941 he wanted to add another corps to it. Hitler turned it down with the argument that it would be better for Italy to concentrate its efforts on North Africa. But he would appreciate a limited contribution of the Italian Alpine-forces, considering the nearby summer offensive in the direction of the Caucasus and Middle East. Mussolini consented with that request enthusiastically. Hitler changed his front after this. On the 29th of December 1941 he wrote Mussolini it was necessary to strengthen the Italian participation to the coming summer offensive in time. This happened because Hitler made higher demands on the dedication of its allies after the recent setback on the eastern front.

Among the European member states of the Tripartite Pact, Bulgaria – because of its pro-Russian feeling within a broad layer of its population – stayed out of the war against the USSR. It did however, as we saw before, join the Anti-Comintern Pact in November 1941. The way this treaty was revitalised at that time was only of propagandistic value.

Amidst Germany's allies it was of course Japan that carried the most weight. Whereas Hitler initially did not appreciate the participation of Japan in the war against the USSR, Ribbentrop insisted, already in the first week of that war, on Japanese intervention against the Soviet Far East. On the 15th of July Hitler met with Oshima, who was told, that the USSR had already been beaten decisively and that the resistance in European Russia would not last any longer than six weeks.

Ribbentrop, who was present at the meeting, was of the opinion that the Soviet government could only be brought down if Japan attacked the USSR, particularly Vladivostok. Hitler added, that in case Japan continued to spare Vladivostok, this by no means would encourage the tendency of the United States to remain non-belligerent. In other words, according to Hitler, it would be better if Japan attacked the USSR, although he did not explicitly insist on it. At that moment Hitler and Mussolini could not know that on the 2nd of July, Japan's imperial conference had decided not to attack the USSR for the time being.

Ribbentrop's fruitless attempts to draw Japan into the war were combined with the German recognition of the satellite government of Wang Ching-wei, which Japan had formed in China. Hitler on the other hand, felt most for

Singapore. Hitler wanted a quick attack of Japan on this city.

a Japanese attack, as soon as possible, in Southeast Asia, particularly Singapore. The sooner it happened, the better its chances would be, he thought. It would be in a position there to obtain the raw materials it would require, especially in case of an American intervention. The longer Japan hesitated, the stronger the United States would become and the more difficult it would be for Japan to complete this campaign. In the autumn of 1941 it became clear that the Japanese military leaders agreed quite a lot with Hitler. For a matter of fact, until the end of August 1941, Hitler was convinced that Japan would attack the USSR at short notice. Although it did not come to that point, this expectation reflected the ambitions of the leaders of the Japanese army. It is true these ambitions were – based on the decision of the 6th of September 1941 – overruled by the emperor, the palace, the 'haute finance' and the navy, but they remained fully focused on a war against the USSR until the attack on Pearl Harbor. Still in July 1941, emperor Hirohito feared that the Kwangtung army would attack the USSR on it's own. On the 14th of July Japan presented the Vichy government a memorandum, in which it demanded the encampment of Japanese troops in South-Indochina. That was accepted a week later. A few days later, Japanese troops landed in South Vietnam. On July 25, the United States proclaimed an oil embargo against Japan, which was initiated by the ABCD nations. Even though Japan had build up oil reserves, acquiescence in the embargo would condemn the country to military and economic paralysis. The navy had enough oil to keep it going for another year and a half, while the army had sufficient for a year. Until now Japan had obtained most of its petroleum from the United States and the remainder from the Dutch East Indies.

The alternative of an agreement with the United States loomed, as a result of which the embargo would be cancelled, or the impossibility of such a compromise. In the latter case Japan would have to provision itself by force, in other words fight a war against the ABCD nations. To put out feelers for the first option, negotiations took place between Ambassador Admiral Nomura and Secretary of State Cordell Hull in Washington in the autumn of 1941. In October, Minister of War Tojo succeeded Prime Minister Konoye. Under his direction the negotiations were combined with the preparations for the jump towards the South.

The fact that the negotiations failed had, as far as Japan is concerned, nothing to do with allied loyalty. On the 19th of November Minister of Foreign Affairs Togo instructed Nomura to inform the American government that Japan,

Prime Minister and Minister of Defence, general Hideki Tojo on his way to his death sentence.

in case of war between another member of the Tripartite Pact and the United States, had the right to stay out of it.

In the preceding month, Tojo (not yet Prime Minister at that time) and chief of staff Sugijama had advised the German government, through ambassador Ott, to look for a political solution with the USSR. This would allow, as was argued, the Japanese-German coalition against the Anglo-Americans to take advantage of the Trans-Siberian railroad. It is remarkable this advice was initiated by two officers of the Japanese land forces, as they were, in general, much more anti-Russian minded than the navy, which of course agreed with Tojo's suggestion. The German regime did not condescend itself to react to the suggestion of the Japanese…

At the negotiations in Washington it was obvious that Japan would have to concede a lot in order to be relieved of the oil-embargo. For a while it seemed that a retreat from Indochina would be sufficient, but the American China lobby opposed that. On the 26th of November Hull presented an announcement that was regarded by Tokyo as an ultimatum. In it, Japan was being thrown back to the status quo of 1931; it had to evacuate the whole of China. On December 7, the Japanese government handed Washington a message that stated negotiations had failed. At that moment the Japanese were bombing the American naval base Pearl Harbor on Hawaii. This surprise attack inflicted heavy losses upon the American fleet in the Pacific.

While Germany had kept the preparations of operation Barbarossa secret to Japan, Japan acted just as discrete. Pearl Harbor was a complete surprise, also in Berlin. But that only concerned this single operation, because at the end of November the Japanese government hinted Berlin of a possible outbreak of war in the Pacific in the short term.

On the 25th of November an imperial conference (chaired by Hirohito) decided that in case the negotiations had not yielded any results by November 25, there would be war. At the same time, considering a probability close to certainty, the following requests were put forward to the German-Italian coalition:

1. Germany and Italy would be automatically at war

with the United States after the breakout of a Japanese-American war. And without the obligation of Japan having to fight the USSR.
2. None of the treaty partners would sign a separate peace.
3. There ought to be a mediation between Germany and Russia.

On the German side, Naval Attaché admiral Wenneker was the first one to be informed. He instructed his superiors in the Navy and the Foreign Office, through Ott. The third suggestion, which we will discuss more than once, did not stand a shadow of a chance with Hitler. In those days Ribbentrop had an illusive view of Japan's jump to the South. He was of the opinion that if Japan would spare the Philippines, it would be able to conquer Singapore without provoking American intervention. The Japanese navy knew better. That's why it attacked Pearl Harbor.

On the 27th of November the German *chargé d'affaires* in Washington, Thomsen, was advised on afore mentioned Cordell Hull-memorandum, which made war inevitable. He informed Ribbentrop, who in turn told a stunned Oshima, who didn't know about it yet. On the 30th of November he received his instructions from Togo. In this document, paragraph 3 of the imperial conference, mediation between Germany and the USSR, had been left out. It did say however, what the answer should be, if asked about Japan's opinion of the USSR. It ought to read that there was no thought of an attack on the USSR for the time being, unless it would join Great Britain and the United States. (Of course this reservation only referred to acts of war in the Far East.)

When Togo's instructions reached the Japanese embassy, Oshima was in Vienna attending a Mozart-festival. Called back by his councillor, he approached Ribbentrop with the request for a prompt German declaration of war and the treaty obligation not to make a separate peace (*Nichtsonderfriedensvertrag*). Ribbentrop was appealed to these suggestions but had to wait with his official permission until Hitler was around. Hitler was in the southern sector of the eastern front, near Rostov, where the situation for the *Wehrmacht* at that time was critical. After Hitler had agreed, Ribbentrop was in a position to officially agree to the Japanese requests on the 5th of December. In the meantime Mussolini had already given his approval on December 3.

Minister Togo used a lie as an argument in this matter. While he made Cordell Hull tell that Japan, in case of an American-German war, would not feel committed to the *casus foederis*, he talked ambassador Ott into believing exactly the opposite. The negotiations in Washington, he suggested, had mainly failed because of the Japanese loyalty to the Tripartite Pact. For this reason the ambassador of the German government expected from its ally full loyalty in return.

On the 5th of December the German government had not been informed yet on the start time of the war in the Pacific. Around that time the Germans proposed that Japan would prevent any further transportation of American supplies to Vladivostok. This was firmly refused by Minister Togo, who furthered détente with the USSR throughout the whole Second World War. On the 7th of December Oshima reported that Germany and Italy had to take on the commitments mentioned earlier before a treaty could be signed. That same day the message of

Mussolini informs his countrymen of the cooperation with Nazi-Germany.

the attack on Pearl Harbor came through via the BBC. Initially Oshima couldn't confirm it to the unbelieving Ribbentrop. In other words, Oshima also had no advance knowledge. When he was in the position to confirm a thing or two, Ribbentrop could inform him that Hitler already had ordered the German navy to attack American ships wherever possible. A few days later the requests of Japan were confirmed in a treaty. Already on the 9th of December China declared war on Japan and Germany. This finally formalised the Japanese-Chinese war that had been dragging on since 1937. Until this moment Japan had referred to this fighting by calling it the 'China incident', a major understatement. Since China had also refrained

Subhas Chandra Bose.

from a declaration of war during those years, the official declaration had to wait until after Pearl Harbor, when it joined the allied camp quite motivated.

The *Nichtsonderfriedensvertrag* between Germany, Italy and Japan was signed December 11. That same day Germany and Italy declared war on the United States. With common warfare in mind – which hardly happened – a military convention was signed between these three on the 18th of January 1942. The border they drew between their areas of operations was illusive, namely the 70th longitude (straight across West-Siberia, East-Afghanistan and

West-British-India), far away from the East European and East Asian stages of war.

A war with the western Allies did not appeal much to the East European member states of the Tripartite Pact. The British government contributed to the solution of that German-Italian problem by declaring war on Romania on December 7, under pressure from the Soviets. Five days later, under pressure from the Germans, followed the Romanian declaration of war on the United States. Antonescu, by now elevated to Field Marshal, reacted to this diplomacy of compulsion by saying the following to a group of journalists on December 12: 'I am an ally of Germany against Russia. I am neutral between Great Britain and Germany. I am for the Americans, against the Japanese.'

In Horthy's Hungary, a more recalcitrant ally than Romania, the resistance against the anti-western obligations of the New Order was even greater. The British government had, considering Operation Barbarossa, broken the relationships with Hungary, without declaring war on that country. In November 1941, the American *chargé d'affaires* handed over a British ultimatum: Hungary had to stop all acts of war before December 5 and withdraw its troops from Soviet territory otherwise a declaration of war would follow. So the British declaration of war on Hungary dates from December 7, as with Romania. One day later the Hungarian government felt impelled to declare war on the United States.

Finland, which didn't join the Tripartite Pact, had a wider margin with the Allies. The Finnish government tried to keep its relations with the Anglo-Americans as normal as possible. These came already under pressure in

July 1941, due to the British-Russian alliance and British air raids in the Petsamo region. Great Britain declared war on Finland on the 6th of December 1941, of course under pressure from the Soviet government.

The inhibitions of the East European regimes, regarding the western democracies, were also based on their concern about the outcome of the German-Russian war. The German offensive against Moscow had resulted in failure and the *Wehrmacht*, including its allies, experienced serious setbacks during the Russian winter.

Between Pearl Harbor and Stalingrad

During the first Russian winter, Mussolini gave again evidence of his *jalousie de métier* towards Hitler, which took, regarding the setbacks on the eastern front, the shape of malicious delight. On the 20th of December 1941, Ciano wrote in his diary: 'Mussolini is rejoiced over the development of the fighting in Russia. He speaks about it openly.' His shy son-in-law added to that 'as long as it doesn't go too far'. On December 28, Ciano again reported something interesting on an issue that he judged otherwise than *Il Duce*: 'Indelli (the Italian ambassador) reports from Tokyo that the Prime Minister of Japan has made some concealed allusions to the possibility of a separate peace between the Axis powers and the USSR. Mussolini has immediately started to investigate the issue and it appeals very much to him.' Also here the latently refractory son-in-law recorded that he didn't believe in the possibility of such a separate peace.

Japan made a tremendous advance in Southeast-Asia during the first months of 1942, which among other things led to the occupation of Malacca (currently Malaysia) and the Dutch East Indies. Especially the fall of the British naval base Singapore was an impressive feat. Hitler, who persistently kept hoping for a *modus vivendi* with the British Empire, showed white grief over these yellow successes. He regretted that the white race was disappearing from Southeast-Asia: 'I didn't want that'. He commented: 'It would have been possible to save East-Asia if all white nations had formed a coalition. Japan wouldn't have been able to do anything against it'. In a fit of wishful thinking, Hitler even alleged that the fall of Singapore would lead to the fall of Churchill and would mean a British about-face in favour of Germany.

Hitler's persistent sympathy for British colonialism is also shown in the following note in the diary of the diplomat Von Hassell, in which the following words were ascribed to Hitler: 'Preferably he would have sent the English twenty divisions to drive those yellow guys back again'. How inhibited Hitler was concerning anti-British policy, is also shown regarding British-India. The Indian nationalist Bose, who, in exile under German and Japanese protection, recruited units from British-Indian prisoners of war to 'liberate' their homeland, was heavily disillusioned in May 1942 with the racist prejudices with which Hitler confronted Indian patriotism. That's why Bose left Germany in February 1943 to try his luck with the Japanese New Order.

This shows there was little real solidarity within the New Order. The two most prominent nations Germany and Japan have never been able to coordinate their strategy, which is proven by their chronic communication disorder in relation to the USSR. This reality was merely poorly covered with the *Nichtsonderfriedensvertrag* and the military convention. The first treaty really filled a gap in the Tripartite Pact, because in the latter the partners didn't guarantee they would refrain from making a separate peace. Furthermore it only committed them to a declaration of war in case any of the allies were attacked, whereas the modifications that were brought forward by Oshima boiled down to an offensive alliance. Therefore Bulgaria, a member of the Tripartite Pact, had been able to abstain from the war against the USSR, without violating the treaty. Of course the same was applicable to Japan. That wasn't an undivided pleasure for the Third Reich. Half of the American aid to the USSR was transported to Vladivostok right under the nose of the Japanese. That was sour for the Germans, while it was worth a lot to Japan; if the USSR had provided the Americans with air force bases in East-Siberia, the bombing of Japan would have started much earlier.

The fact that Japan already undertook attempts in the autumn of 1941 to realise a German-Russian peace, was mainly Togo's work. This former ambassador in both Berlin and Moscow acted as Minister of Foreign Affairs from October 1941 until September 1942. In November 1941, during the liaison conference of the emperor, ministers and senior officers of army and navy, he proposed to push Hitler for making peace with Stalin before a summer offensive would be possible. The military leaders were of opinion that Germany would win the war and were planning an attack on the Soviet Far East. The chief of the general staff, Sugijama, claimed that Japan could only recommend a separate peace to Germany, if the upcoming German summer offensive would end in a disaster. Nevertheless, in January 1942 Togo handed the parting

Soviet ambassador in Tokyo, Smetanin, the message that in case the Soviet government wanted peace, Japan would be happy to mediate. In view of the above mentioned liaison conference, which must have been a typical Japanese example of trespassing on competence. Togo wrote his memoirs in an allied prison shortly after the end of the Second Word War, therefore undocumented. This may explain why his book is incomplete with regard to the information below.

When operation Barbarossa started, a certain general Tatekawa was Japanese ambassador in Moscow. After he was called back from Moscow, in 1942, he highly praised the military capacities and prospects of the USSR. This annoyed ambassador Ott and also irritated Hitler, Ribbentrop and Goebbels. Therefore the Japanese Ministry of Foreign Affairs called him to order; he had to weaken his high opinion of the Soviet army.

The earlier mentioned quotation from Ciano's diary that the Japanese Prime Minister had made an allusion towards a German-Russian peace, actually referred to a former Prime Minister, Konoye. He did discuss these matters with Inelli, the Italian ambassador in Tokyo. Mussolini was appealed to it, but didn't consider it opportune to discuss this with Hitler.

In March 1942, the Japanese naval staff sent an envoy to the German naval attaché, admiral Wenneker, to offer Japanese mediation in aid of a German-Russian peace, since Germany was more or less bleeding to death on the eastern front. Wenneker reported about this enthusiastically to his superior *Grossadmiral* Raeder, who would then recommend this proposal to Hitler. The only result was that Wenneker was seriously reprimanded because of this message, which was considered defeatist and absurd. The Japanese army leaders still followed the example of the navy in June 1942. For this reason they planned a mission to Berlin, which wasn't followed up by Ribbentrop and Oshima. Subsequently the initiator, colonel Tsuji, told ambassador Ott, on behalf of the disappointed Japanese officers, that initiatives of this kind would not happen anymore unless the German government requested them. Apparently Minister Togo had different thoughts about that, because in July 1942 he gave instructions to Sato (who had succeeded Tatekawa as ambassador to the Soviet Union) to promote a German-Russian peace. Sato answered that he didn't see an opportunity for that at this time. Togo himself now decided to travel to Moscow – supposedly for negotiations on a fishing agreement – but before it came to that, he resigned over a dispute on competence.

The fact that, in the summer of 1942, so much was undertaken by the Japanese to arrange an end to the German-Russian war was probably linked with the heavy defeat of the Japanese fleet near the Midway-islands in June 1942. It underlined once again, that Japan, like Italy, would greatly benefit from a concentration of the German potential against the western Allies. The Japanese defeat near the Midway-islands weighed very heavily. It meant the turning point of the war in the Pacific came a few months earlier than in Europe and North Africa.

In the meantime, the Japanese interferences to mediate a German-Russian peace also didn't make a shadow of a chance in the Kremlin. Stalin informed the United States about these Japanese initiatives. That was probably favourable for the magnitude of the American arms and other supplies to the USSR.

Nazi-Germany is working on the Tripartite Pact. Hitler is having a conversation with the Hungarian Prime Minister Teleki, November 1940. In the middle press officer Dr. Dietrich. On the right: Bormann, Von Schirach and Von Erdmannsdorff.

The Soviet spy Sorge was arrested in Tokyo in October 1941. The last service he rendered the Kremlin was invaluable. He reported the Japanese priority of the jump towards the South, which enabled Stalin to deploy troops from the Far East near Moscow. Without the messages from Sorge the USSR would not have been able to do that, because in the months after the beginning of Barbarossa the strength of the Kwangtung-army had been increased from 400 thousand to 700 thousand men. Without the intelligence of Sorge this would have given the Soviet leaders the worst possible fears. The reinforcement of the Kwangtung-army shows that Japan could have attacked the USSR without having to fear a harmful cutting up of its capabilities. The Kwangtung-army remained in Manchukuo until August 1945, although its strength had been decreased since 1943 in order to support the offensives against the Kuomintang forces. The reinforcements this army went through in 1941 were apparently only carried through in case the USSR was totally beaten in Europe. They thought that even in that case – bearing the lessons learned at Nomonhan in mind (page 31) - they would have to line up with substantial armed forces.

In November 1942 ambassador Ott was dismissed. Ribbentrop motivated this with the exposure of Sorge, who indeed had been a frequent guest at the German embassy. But since the arrest of Sorge more than a year had passed. In reality it was about something completely different. In his role as attaché, admiral Wenneker would come directly under the High Command of the Armed Forces. Within the framework of the internal struggle of competence, a position was being removed from Ribbentrop's domain. The vain foreign minister was compensated with Ott's dismissal. The ambassador had shown so much displeasing expertise that Ribbentrop was quite happy to replace him with the subservient Stahmer, who would always report what suited his boss best. The combination Ribbentrop-Stahmer later turned out to be one that would cause major damage.

The setbacks on the eastern front that hit Germany during the winter war of 1941-1942 had by now led to a situation in which Hitler and his officers made a heavier call upon their European allies. This was expressed in the letters he wrote to Mussolini, Antonescu and Horthy around the turn of the year. In these letters he pretended that the coming summer offensive would lead to the final liquidation of Bolshevism. Hitler also promised that the Italian, Romanian and Hungarian troops would be brought into action under their own commanders. All three allies showed compliancy. Mussolini did not only send more troops for reasons of prestige, but also to persuade the Germans to make less use of the Italian *Arbeitseinsatz* (imported workforce).

Antonescu demanded three things with regard to his promised efforts:

1. A German guarantee against further Hungarian and Bulgarian requests for territory;
2. Hungary would also have to increase its efforts;
3. The equipment of the Romanian troops had to be improved.

Romania received the requested guarantees in every respect, but regarding paragraph 3 Germany failed terribly. The Romanian troops continued to suffer from considerable shortages of tanks and anti-tank weapons. This was also the case with the Italian and Hungarian forces. There was a difference between the Romanian and Hungarian efforts; in 1942 two thirds of the Romanian troops were fighting on the eastern front against one third of the Hungarian. Antonescu kept hoping that he would be able to outplay Hungary within the New Order, in other words to convince Germany into reviewing the second *Wiener Schiedsspruch*. Romania and Hungary kept arguing over their minorities (a Romanian minority in Hungary and a Hungarian minority in Romania), as well as over the border demarcation in Northern Transylvania. A bloody incident took place there in October 1942. No wonder the Germans couldn't trust the Romanians and Hungarians to fight shoulder to shoulder on the eastern front. For this reason Italian troops were placed between Hungarian and Romanian units. Towards the autumn of 1942, the *Wehrmacht* concentrated itself on Stalingrad that was being strongly defended, while the sectors north and south of the 'Volga knee bend' were left, for a considerable part, to Hungarian, Italian and Romanian troops. After the Soviet offensive that led to the encirclement of the German troops in Stalingrad had started, their allied forces retreated quickly. Here and there it was quite panicky. This led to severe criticism from the Germans on the Italian, Romanian and Hungarian troops. The allied leaders didn't have a problem coming up with an answer. Particularly the Romanians pointed out that the Germans had not kept their promise regarding equipment. The allies resisted the German tendency to turn them into the scapegoats that were responsible for the defeats the New Order suffered in the autumn and winter of 1942-1943.

The decisive German defeat at Stalingrad reinforced the tendency of the Finnish, Hungarian and Romanian regimes to probe the possibilities of an agreement with the western Allies that would protect them against subjection by the USSR.

Bulgaria remained a privileged satellite state, since it didn't have to fight a war against the USSR. That exceptional position was based on the pro-Russian feelings among its population. In addition the government used the argument that the Russians might land on the coast of Bulgaria; therefore it was wiser to leave the troops at home. The Germans benefited from the Bulgarian troops that helped to oppress Serbia, Macedonia and Greece. In December 1941 the Bulgarian government felt impelled to declare war on the United States and Great Britain.

Additionally they had to accept German demands with respect to measures against Jews and communists.

Despite its membership of the Anti-Comintern Pact, Finland persevered in a separate policy. Having to endure a British declaration of war under these circumstances was a heavy blow for Finland's relatively independent warfare. The entry of the United States into the war also made a deep impression. Furthermore commander-in-chief Mannerheim was very pessimistic. He feared that the situation on the eastern front would end in a disaster. During those days the United States made it clear to the Finnish authorities that they could only count on American goodwill if they would stop their offensive actions against the USSR. This applied especially to the Murmansk railroad, which was essential for the American aid to the Soviet warfare. Mannerheim put proposals of the German Supreme Command about a German-Finnish winter offensive quietly aside.

On his 75th birthday, on June 4 1942, Hitler paid him a flying visit. On this occasion Hitler's language – and he better improve! – was more professional than usual.

He admitted shortcomings in the German warfare and confessed in having misjudged the potential of the Soviets. Hitler also claimed that he actually had not wanted this war and regretted that the German Reich had not been in a position to assist Finland in the Winter War (1939-1940). Next, the German government enjoyed the satisfaction that the Allies were annoyed with Mannerheim's return visit to the *Führerhauptquartier*.

The fact that Finland was spared by Germany had, according to Wegner, three reasons:

1. Hitler respected the 'heroic people' of Finland;

2. Because of Germany's concentration on the southern front, Finland wasn't that important;
3. Hitler wanted to spare the Finnish army, as he feared an allied landing operation in North-Norway.

The latter indicates he did not suspect that the Finnish authorities – like the Hungarians – were flirting with the allies.

Now that the southern front prevailed, 1942 had not been so dramatic for Finland. Italy had suffered heavy losses on that front, but was less demoralised by it than Hungary and Romania. As a result of the Anglo-American advance, which occurred in North Africa since October 1942, the Italians were more focused on Mediterranean operations. That was the reason that Mussolini shared the Japanese view concerning the USSR. He had made this known to general Von Rintelen, the German liaison officer at the Italian headquarters. The following month, instructed by Mussolini, Ciano tried to persuade Hitler into a compromise with the USSR, which *Der Führer* rejected out of hand. Mussolini's concept of 'a new Brest-Litovsk-treaty' – referring to the unbearable peace Germany had imposed upon Soviet Russia in March 1918 – was an illusion; Stalin would never fall for that.

The cries for a separate peace within the New Order never felt silent after Stalingrad. By far most of Germany's allies were of the opinion that it had bitten off more than it could chew. But relating this matter – as we have seen – no agreement could be reached between the nations that feared the most of the USSR and the Japanese-Italian tendency of aiming at a concentration of power against the western Allies.

On the way to the end

In March 1943 the Germans, on their own, had succeeded in stabilising their eastern front. In the meantime they kept blaming the Italian, Hungarian and Romanian troops that the defeat at Stalingrad was due to their failure. Related to this, the German chief of staff Zeitzler said about the European allies: 'I never want to see them again'. In reality these allies, as we saw, were poorly equipped and the front lines north and south of Stalingrad were occupied far too long and too thin. Hitler had helped the Soviet strategy by his prestigious concentration on the city on the Volga. The afore mentioned feelers of peace that Germany's European allies put out towards the western Allies gave of course much offence in Berlin. Antonescu and Horthy left the diplomatic reconnaissance to their ministers Mihai Antonescu (no family) and Kallay. The intention was to agree to such a peace with the West that the Russians would be kept outside. That design was not feasible; the British kept the USSR informed and avoided any diplomatic manoeuvre which could lead to a crack in the anti-Hitler coalition.

In December 1942 the collapse of the 4th Romanian army had coincided with the escape to Italy of the leader of the Iron Guard, Horia Sima, who had been interned in Germany. After he had been captured and brought back to Germany, marshal Antonescu demanded his extradition. Hitler refused that, contrary to a promise he made earlier. In April 1943 this strongly contributed to the suspicious atmosphere in which the visit of a Romanian delegation to the *Führerhauptquartier* took place. Hitler answered Marshal Antonescu's complaints, regarding insults by German military personnel about their Romanian colleagues, by calling them a common phenomenon, namely the rough language that was typical of soldiers who had been on the front. During this meeting Hitler again repulsed the idea of a separate peace. He was committed to perseverance in the fight against all enemies.

Mihai Antonescu, who had returned from East Prussia very pessimistically, contacted his friend Bova Scoppa, the Italian envoy in Bucharest, again. During the last autumn, both men had taken on the idea of a 'Latin Axis', meaning a bloc of Italy, France, Spain, Portugal and Romania, which would keep Germany under control and turn the tide against the Slavic countries. Both Romania and Hungary were inclined to have Italy, on behalf of Germany's other European allies, take the lead in an attempt to persuade Hitler in making peace with the west. Bova Scoppa handed, on the basis of the recent Romanian experiences with Hitler, a memorandum to Ciano to influence Mussolini in that direction. After an initially favourable reaction of *Il Duce*, he turned around completely by saying that he would stick to his common destiny with Germany. All of this happened in January 1943. The following month Ciano was dismissed.

Mussolini's statement that he would follow Germany until the end looked – in view of his plea for an arrangement with the USSR – a lot like a pose. Mihai Antonescu had nothing to expect from Italian diplomacy. Subsequently he tried to convince the western Allies, by making use of neutral countries, how dangerous the Bolshevist advance would be for Europe. But also this was a dead end street, considering the Anglo-American loyalty towards the USSR. In 1943 Germany has substantially decreased the use of allied troops on the eastern front. At the same time it had to keep its allies under control, which was, consider-

Tokio showing the signs of cooperation with Hitler and Mussolini.

ing the German military superiority, feasible for the time being. Romania remained vital for economic reasons, Hungary as well, but to a lesser extent and Italy had to tolerate compulsory recruitment for the *Arbeitseinsatz* on a large scale. Since Romania was economically of essential importance, it suffered most under the German exploitation.

In January 1943 both Antonescu's were put under heavy pressure. Germany complained that this past year, Romania's internal consumption of petroleum had increased with 25%, whereas the export to Germany had decreased from 3.9 million ton to 3.3 million ton. The Romanians complained about the enormous shortage on Germany's balance of trade. Germany promised to secure that shortage partly with gold and to help the nineteen Romanian divisions in getting better equipment by 1944. Romania, on the other hand, would be committed to supply Germany with 4 million ton of oil a year.

In March 1943 Kallay visited Rome. He was sensible enough not to talk to Mussolini about a separate peace with the western Allies. Kallay hoped to utilize the influence of *Il Duce* on Hitler, for a revision of the politics of the Axis powers in aid of more influence for Germany's allies. To discuss this he suggested a conference of the European members of the Tripartite Pact. Also that didn't stand a chance. Given Germany's predominance over and suspicion of its allies, there was little to discuss and a lot to dictate for Hitler. With that in mind Mussolini, Antonescu and Horthy were successively summoned to Klessheim castle (Salzburg) in April 1943. In his letter of the 16th of March 1943 to Hitler, Mussolini had again insisted upon a separate peace with the USSR. This was discussed in Klessheim, but Hitler didn't give in. Ribbentrop told his Italian colleague, Ciano's successor Bastianini, that Hungary and Romania, bringing up the topic of peace negotiations, had attacked the German soldiers from behind, something that would not be tolerated under any circumstances. Upon his arrival, Mussolini was tormented with gastric cramps and had Hitler win him over once again. The German leader assured him that Tunesia had been recreated into a bastion that would be impregnable for the Allies. The following month also that area had to be surrendered. With that it became clear that it would now be Italy's turn during the Anglo-American campaign.

When subsequently Antonescu and Horthy paid their respect in Klessheim castle, they were put under pressure to fire their Ministers of Foreign Affairs. This was refused, which wasn't a miracle, because both Antonescu and Horthy knew all the ins and outs about their most important diplomats. Hitler and Ribbentrop interpreted the Hungarian and Romanian contacts with the western Allies as criminal symptoms of weakness. The German leaders had lesser problems with Croatia and Slovakia. The satellite regimes in those countries remained loyal to the New Order until the Allies occupied them in 1944 and 1945.

The first defection took place in Italy, in July 1943. On the 10th of that month the Anglo-Americans landed on Sicily. Mihai Antonescu had visited Mussolini a week and a half earlier. The Romanian minister came with the proposal that Italy, Romania and Hungary would end the war at the same time and on the initiative of *Il Duce*. During those days the Italian leader was sick, passive, sleepy and not capable anymore of taking any initiative. Mussolini's next meeting with Hitler became the prologue of his dismissal. His chief of staff Ambrosio had made it very clear to him that Italy had no energy left and it therefore had to end the war as well as cancel its alliance. This time the Italians stipulated that the conference would take place in their country. It happened in the northern town of Feltre. Also at this occasion Mussolini was completely overwhelmed by Hitler's flood of words and didn't he pass on Ambrosio's urgent message. After the conference Mussolini told Ambrosio that he would inform Hitler about the abovementioned message by letter. The chief of staff answered that it would have been better if *Il Duce* had passed the message on in Feltre, since a letter would not be answered. Additionally Ambrosio, who was despondent and didn't want to be responsible for a continuation of the war any longer, handed in his resignation.

The top of the fascist establishment was now also convinced that it couldn't go on like this. On the evening of the 24th of July, the supreme board of the party, the 'Great Fascist Council' assembled. During that meeting the former diplomat Grandi drew up a plan to have king Victor Emanuel III, who previously was regarded a dummy of *Il Duce*, succeed Mussolini as commander in chief. This vote of no confidence was accepted with a considerable majority. The verbal defence of the heavily disconcerted leader was insignificant. The next day, at his audience with the king, the latter informed him that he was dismissed and would be succeeded by marshal Badoglio. Mussolini was promptly arrested after his exit.

The coup meant the collapse of fascism. Marshall Badoglio pretended that Italy was continuing the war at the side of the Germans, but at the same time secretly negotiated about a cease-fire with the allies. On the 3rd of September the Italian government secretly signed its capitulation. It was made public on September 8, on the day the allies – which had occupied Sicily in the meantime – landed near Salerno (south of Naples). Badoglio requested a postponement of the announcement in order to better prepare for the inevitable German intervention. The Anglo-Americans haven't agreed to that request. The

Germans took over North and Middle-Italy. They disarmed most of the Italian troops there and on the Balkan. Badoglio and the King fled to Brindisi and declared war on Germany in October 1943. This resulted in two Italian regimes. The Germans 'freed' Mussolini. They installed him in the North as the leader of a republican fascist satellite regime.

Shortly after Mussolini was overthrown, the competent trouble-shooter Rahn became German ambassador in Rome. Since Rome came under direct German military rule and Mussolini's regime resided in the north, also Rahn's location became Lake Garda. The next twenty months Mussolini was under the tactful guardianship of Rahn, who showed some understanding for the flipped dictator, but could not spare him any humiliations. Rahn did not believe in the *Endsieg* (final victory) anymore. When Ribbentrop had offered him this assignment, he had characterised his instructions as those of an assignee in bankruptcy.

Now that the monarchy had committed 'treason', the fascist party was re-established in republican form. The fascist satellite state was called the 'Republic of Salo', because of her northern residence. In December 1943 it took on the name *Republica Sociale Italiana*. The 'social' aspect of it was a little bit more than just an empty phrase. Under the remaining fascists a fierce resentment had grown against the old establishment: the court, aristocracy and 'haute bourgeoisie', especially entrepreneurs. Because of that they came with plans to nationalise industries, which were established by law. Hitler hadn't actually made any objections against it, but among the German resorts in Italy – afraid of a destabilisation of the weapon industry

– these red temptations of the young republic were effectively sabotaged. Mussolini had announced former leftist fantasies – including proletarian participation – in his radio speech of the 18th of September 1943, during which he debunked 'plutocracy'.

The biggest humiliation fascist Italy suffered was the fact that *Gauleiter* (district leaders) were brought into action in the northern border provinces; they did not care about the Italian Republic at all, which in reality boiled down to German annexation. The German were fond of Italian forced labour and entrusted the Social Republic with little military resources. They had the most confidence in the Republican Guard, which assisted in the fight against the, mostly communist, partisans. After the capitulation of the Badoglio government, the Germans disarmed around seven hundred thousand Italian soldiers and utilized most of them as forced labourer. The political and economical collapse of Italy meant that a large part of the Italian arms on the Balkan fell into the hands of the Yugoslav, Greek and Albanian partisans.

The Republic of Salo was of course a pathetic display. Officially Mussolini's ramshackle restored regime still belonged to the Tripartite Pact. That's why already in September 1943 Ribbentrop instructed his allies to proceed with the recognition of this government, which happened. Romania, Bulgaria, Croatia and Slovakia showed their willingness, but in the case of Hungary, which was quite rebellious, pressure was necessary. Japan joined in as well, apparently to keep the New Order, which was caving in, together. In January 1944 a number of leading fascists, including Ciano, were condemned to death and executed because of their actions that past July.

In April 1944 Mussolini and Hitler met each other once again at Klessheim castle. During this meeting Mussolini claimed that his regime had accomplished quite a lot. He also admitted that only a minority of the Italian population supported his regime. According to him the majority stood between 'scepticism and pessimism'. Apparently that was something different than anti, because he added that 'only a few plutocratic aristocrats' opposed his regime. He also said that his regime required more independence in order to gain more credibility with the Italian population. Hitler complained about the Italian workers in Germany. Even the French workers 'behave themselves better'. He also complained about Hungary and Romania, which, according to him, wanted to spare their own troops in order to start a 'private war', obviously referring to their conflict over Northern Transylvania. He added that he had felt the obligation to take necessary measures against Hungary. It had pursued an agreement with Badoglio and also had the tendency to chum up with the British and Americans.

Hitler's statement about Hungary wasn't far from the truth and had given him enough reason for an armed intervention. After Mussolini was brought down, Kallay got wind of the Italian negotiations with the Allies. In Budapest they hoped to be in a position to follow that diplomatic example. In principle they were willing to accept a capitulation, provided there were sufficient western troops around to prevent a subjection of the country by the Nazi's (or the Russians). As mentioned before, the Anglo-Americans didn't want to take any action without involving the USSR. After the Italian capitulation, the Hungarians hoped that the Allies, through a landing near Istria, would soon be closer than the Russians. The Germans didn't fail to notice these negotiations between Hungarian and British diplomats.

Already in 1943 Ribbentrop had sent the economist Veesenmayer to Hungary to observe the suspected Horthy-regime. His reports tended to a suspicious pessimism. In February 1944 German intelligence scented that Kallay had asked for Anglo-American airborne troops and had also stuck out its antennas in the direction of Moscow. Additionally Horthy wrote Hitler the same month that he wanted to withdraw Hungarian troops from the eastern front. For this reason Hitler decided to invade and occupy Hungary in March 1944. When Horthy paid a call on Hitler at Klessheim castle once again during that month, he was confronted with the accomplished fact that German troops were entering his country. Horthy got into a rage, but was persuaded to summon the pro-German envoy in Berlin, Sztojay, to become Prime Minister. Horthy could remain in office and the German troops were partly withdrawn. Veesenmayer now got the same position in Hungary, which Rahn occupied in Italy. The economic exploitation of the country (petroleum, bauxite, food supplies) was intensified and outside Budapest the deportation of Jews to the gas chambers had started. The Horthy regime would nevertheless remain a protesting ally for a few more months.

At the same time it got worse and worse with the German warfare. On the 4th of June Rome had to be given up. In August 1944 the western Allies conquered France, while the Red Army completed the conquest of the Ukraine and invaded Romania. The Soviet advance resulted in the overthrow of Antonescu's regime. That regime was authoritarian, but far from totalitarian. Although there was a one party system, there was some space for the agrarian leader Maniu and his liberal colleague Bratianu. In the summer of 1943 marshal Antonescu had declined their peace interferences. His argument: a capitulation (another cease-fire wasn't possible) for the Allies would lead to a German regime of occupation. In that case the Germans would confiscate the Romanian inventories of petrol and grain without having to pay for it. The German Reich would also deprive Romania of Southern Transylvania and North-Dobrudzha in order to hand them over to Hungary and Bulgaria respectively. Around the turn of the year of 1943-1944 the Romanian envoy in Stockholm, Nanu, had various meetings with Soviet diplomats. In February Nanu reported that the USSR would respect the sovereignty of Romania and would cooperate in regaining Northern Transylvania. Mihai Antonescu didn't react to it in order to concentrate on the western Allies. Subsequently negotiations with the British took place in Cairo, which were initiated by Nanu. They made it clear to their interlocutor, prince Barbu Stirbey, that Romania would not be able to avoid an unconditional capitulation. When marshal Antonescu paid his respects at Klessheim castle in March 1944, Hitler was fully aware of the negotiations that had taken place in Cairo. In order to keep Romania within the German camp, Antonescu was told that Germany no longer recognised the second *Wiener Schiedspruch* and would shortly summon the Hungarian troops in Northern Transylvania to evacuate that area. That evacuation was not to be enforced until six months later, as a result of the Soviet advance.

In April 1944 the Red Army reached the Pruth, the Romanian border of 1941. Barbu Stirbey received a summary of the Soviet demands in Cairo; break with Germany, join the Allies, unlimited access of the Soviet troops and reparations. But they also added a pleasant message: the annulment of the *Wiener Schiedspruch*, which meant regaining Northern Transylvania. Marshal Antonescu rejected these terms of capitulation. In the meantime agrarian, liberal, social-democratic and communist parties had constituted a National Democratic Bloc, which, floating between illegality and legalisation, formed a front against the regime. On the 20th of August the major Soviet offensive started. While the German troops managed to continue the battle, the Romanian resistance collapsed. On August 23, king Michaël invited Antonescu for a meeting. When the marshal, during his visit to the palace, refused to announce a cease-fire, he was arrested together with Mihai Antonescu. General Sanatescu, who had organised the royal coup, formed a coalition government. During a radio speech king Michaël announced the cease-fire with the allies and the break with Germany. The Russians got free play in Romania from a military point of view, although it took until 1947 before the communist pattern of rule was completed. The German troops were no match for the combined Russian-Romanian attacks, which implied they had evacuated most of the country by early September. On the 24th of August the Germans presented Horia Sima, who had previously been interned by them. That became a disaster. His bluff that he had seventy thousand followers at his disposal in Romania, who would start a guerrilla, turned out to be a failure. Sima aroused so much resistance within the remaining territory under German control that it took until the 10th of December 1944, before he was in a position to create a 'national government' in exile. The only things this group was occupied with, were propaganda as well as the Romanian prisoner of wars and workers in Germany. It was a remarkable phenomenon that Romanian soldiers who had fought alongside the Germans for over three years were now available for action against their former allies. That Romania declared war on Hungary wasn't a surprise. It goes without saying that there were heavy fights in order to regain Northern Transylvania. The Romanians suffered huge losses. In the war against the USSR around 300 thousand soldiers were killed, whereas the later fight against the Germans claimed 169 thousand more victims. That is quite a lot for a country that had a population of around 16 million in 1940.

The Soviet conquest of Romania threatened to make the situation in Hungary unbearable. In spite of the German occupation and the fact that they had enforced the role of Sztojay as Prime Minister, Horthy kept raising objections. For example in June 1944 he sent Hitler a letter in which he protested against the actions of the SS and the Gestapo who behaved like hostile occupiers. Horthy managed to get rid of Sztojay in August. During his diplomatic explorations in the direction of the Anglo-Americans, there was no other alternative left, after the Russian conquest of Transylvania, than to send a delegation to Moscow with the objective of achieving a ceasefire. On the 11th of October they agreed to a capitulation which wasn't made public at that time. This also included a declaration of war against Germany. Horthy, who didn't want to attack his ally in the back, refused to execute this requirement. Before the capitulation could be carried out,

German elite forces had arrested Horthy. He was interned in Germany. After this quickly executed coup the Germans put the exalted and muddle-headed Szálasi in power. When he still served under Horthy, this leader of the fascist Arrow Cross party had to be satisfied with a role in the opposition. Most of the Jews that lived outside Budapest had already been deported to the gas chambers. But now an enormously cruel murder campaign of members of the Arrow Cross party against the Jews of Budapest broke out. Hungary was the last stage of action during the Second World War, where a major German offensive took place. After the Soviets had conquered Budapest, which resulted in heavy losses on both sides, the last offensive convulsion of the Third Reich happened in March 1945. In April 1945 – more than six months after Romania - the Russians had finally completely occupied Hungary. The losses on the Hungarian side were just as catastrophic as they were for Romania. Around 300 thousand Hungarians lost their life during the war at the eastern front. Apart from that, around one fifth of the 600 thousand military and civilians who ended up in Soviet camps died as a result of the hardship's inflicted upon them. As a result of the exodus of the German minority and the genocide of the Jews Hungary became a mono-ethnic country. That was quite a heavy loss on a population of 14.7 million in 1941. The end of the New Order in the member countries of the Anti-Comintern Pact and Tripartite Pact, Croatia, Slovakia and Bulgaria had nothing to do with the pursuit of a separate peace. The satellite regimes of Germany in these countries were eliminated without any diplomatic complications as a result of the Soviets advance. Their replacement by communist regimes is another story, which is part of the prologue and history of the Cold War. Finland came out of it a lot better. It remained preserved from a German occupation and a communist future. In April 1943, an offer of the United Stated to mediate between Finland and the USSR was turned down under German pressure. The declaration that Finland would not pursue a separate peace, which was enforced by Ribbentrop, wasn't given until a year later. This promise expired after President Ryti stepped down (August 1, 1944). Under his successor Mannerheim the course was set for a cease-fire. In the meantime the Germans had already stopped their deliveries of grain and weapons. Early September 1944 the German government was informed about the end of the Finnish war. As a result of this it was stated that the German forces had to leave the country by the 15th of September. Any soldiers that remained after that date would be disarmed and extradited. Finland broke its relations with Germany. The attempt of the Germans to keep the North occupied, failed. The Germans had to leave from there in October. The position of brother-in-arms had turned into bitterness. Finland was spared from an entry of the Red Army.

During the years of the collapse of power, which followed Stalingrad, the relations between Japan and Germany didn't really get the character of coalition warfare. After all, both nations were kept far apart by the USSR, both geographically and diplomatically! Germany's diplomatic mission in Tokyo had, in the meantime, lost a lot of quality as a result of the appointment of Stahmer. We already came across this person regarding his peculiar role at the realisation of the Tripartite Pact (page 297). He systematically reported what suited Ribbentrop best.

On the 21st of April, Japan got a new Minister of Foreign Affairs, Shigemitsu. In front of Stahmer he criticised the German warfare, including its policy of occupation, and intensified the attempts to arrange a German-Russian peace. Stahmer failed to pass this criticism over to Ribbentrop. That didn't help much, because Oshima, who remained persistently Nazi oriented, felt impelled to pass on Shigemitsu's messages.

While Japan, in 1943, continued its efforts in favour of a German-Russian peace, Stalin kept loyally reporting that to the United States. Goebbels and Ribbentrop felt for it, but Hitler held on to his veto. At the same time Ribbentrop kept desperately insisting upon an intervention of Japan against the USSR. In order to accomplish this, he resorted, in October 1943, to an obtuse form of disinformation. He concocted an intelligence message that contained the following nonsense: the Soviet Far East would have been stripped from a military point of view, because a million soldiers from that territory had been directed to Europe, while the Asian part of the USSR had been flooded with workers from Persia, India and China, which made this territory indefensible. When Ribbentrop handed this disinformation to Oshima, he didn't believe it, but still said he would pass it on to his superiors. This happened on the 3rd of October 1943. It made the German military attaché in Tokyo, general Kretschmer, desperate and furious. In a message to the Supreme Command of the Army he reported, on October 11, that the Japanese general staff regarded this so-called intelligence only as a symptom of the extremely weak position of the Germans against the Soviet forces. The Japanese made it clear to the Germans that their position on the eastern front was hopeless and that in order to accomplish peace, it would be necessary to give the Ukraine back to the USSR. This was out-of-date at this moment, because the Red Army enforced the evacuation of the Ukraine a few months later. Goebbels understood that. He was willing to offer the USSR Eastern Europe as a sphere of influence – including North-Norway, Finland and Greece – but Hitler didn't like this fantastic suggestion at all. The Japanese, who had joined the Anti-Comintern Pact with such an anticommunist zeal, have for such a long time persisted in their attempts for peace because they underestimated Hitler's escalating drive towards death. They weren't able to recognise that psychiatric problem.

The German reports from Tokyo, in the meantime, were characterized by on the contrast between Stahmer and Wenneker. The first one voiced optimistic phrases, whereas the admiral gave a down-to-earth account of the superior strength of the Americans.

The Japanese leaders expected in February 1945 that the German empire would collapse around the middle of the year. After the capitulation of Germany, Togo, who once again had become Minister of Foreign Affairs, protested to Stahmer against the German violation of the clause not to conclude an armistice or peace on its own. He withdrew his protest, when Stahmer explained him there was no alternative solution. Japan needlessly cancelled all treaties with the non-existent German empire. All German missions and organisations in Japan were now dissolved and all Germans that lived there were interned.

The conclusion of Bernd Wegner

The German historian Bernd Wegner published an article

in which he argues that Hitler didn't believe in the *Endsieg* (final victory) anymore after 1942 and subsequently completely focused on the 'heroism of the downfall'. He would have recognised the inevitable victory of the Allies and followed a theatrical scenario that had to bring about an enormous posthumous effect. His scenario towards self-destruction could only be executed if the Germans and their allies would continue to fight until their last gasp. In order to realise that, Hitler had covered his expectations of defeat with encouraging fictions of disagreements within the coalition of the enemy, as well as other daydreams and propaganda. That would have been manipulation to keep the shrinking New Order in Europe on course. In other words, it would have taken deceit to satisfy Hitler's *Lust um Untergang,* the most fitting German characterisation, signifying the urge to death and destruction.

I believe Wegner is right. His supporting evidence is convincing. It also explains why Hitler wasn't accessible with any peace proposals after 1942. From that moment on all peace proposals to Germany were doomed to fail. But there was more than just one dictator. It seems to me that the New Order was too diverse anyway to keep to one diplomatic course. It wasn't possible to form a 'Fascintern' with such a diversity of extreme nationalists. Internationalism of chauvinists is just as imaginary as vegetarian tigers…

Bibliography

M. Bloch, *Ribbentrop*, Bantam Press Londen 1992.
R. Bohr, *Stalin's rugdekking*, in Intermediair jg. 33 18 aug. 1989.
M. Boog c.s., *Der Angriff auf die Sowjetunion*, Fischer Taschenbuch Verlag Frankfurt 1991.
P. Calvocoressi, G. Wint & J. Pritchard, *The Causes and Courses of the Second World War*, Penguin Books Harmondsworth 1989.
A. Cassels, *Fascist Italy*, Routledge & Kegan London 1969.
Ciano's dagboek, Arbeiderspers Amsterdam 1947.
A. D. Coox, *Nomonhan-Japan against Russia 1939*, Stanford University Press 1985.
Ibid., *The Unfought War-Japan 1941-1942*, San Diegos State University Press 1992.
F.W. Deakin, *The Brutal Friendship*, Penguin Books Harmondsworth 1962.
H. von Dirksen, *Moskau, Tokyo, Londen*, Kohlhammer Stuttgart 1949.
J. Förster, *Die Auswirkungen der Katastrophe von Stalingrad 1942/43 auf die Verbündeten Deutschlands und der Türkei*, thesis Cologne University, Rombach Freiburg 1975.
M. Funke (editor), *Hitler, Deutschland und die Mächte*, Athenäum/Droste Düsseldorf 1978.
F. Genoud (editor), *The Testament of Adolf Hitler*, Cassell London 1959.
J. Göbbels, *Tagebücher 1924-1945*, vol. 4 1940-'42, Piper Munich 1992.
P. Gosztony, *Miklos von Horthy*, Musterschmidt Göttingen 1973.
K. Hildebrand, *Deutsche Aussenpolitik 1933-1945*, Kohlhammer Stuttgart 1980.

A. Hillgruber, *Hitler, König Carol und Marschall Antonescu*, Musterschmidt Göttingen 1954.

Ibid., *Hitlers Strategie*, Bernard & Graefe Verlag für Wehrwesen Frankfurt 1965.

Ibid., *Staatsmänner und Diplomaten bei Hitler*, Deutscher Taschenbuch Verlag Munich 1969.

Ibid., *Sowjetische Aussenpolitik im Zweiten Weltkrieg*, Droste Verlag Düsseldorf 1979.

K. Hitchins, *Romania 1866-1947*, Clarendon Press Oxford 1994.

A. Hitler, *Mein Kampf*, Verlag Franz Eher Munich 1933.

J. Horn & E. Sira, *Het Italiaans fascisme*, van Gorcum Assen 1980.

A. Iriye, *The Origins of the Second World War in Asia and the Pacific*, Longman London 1987.

B. Jelavich, *History of the Balkans*, vol. 2 Cambridge University Press 1983.

F. C. Jones, *Japan's New Order in East Asaia*, Oxford University Press 1960.

G. K. Kindermann, *Der Ferne Osten*, DTV Weltgeschichte des 20. Jahrhunderts vol. 6, Deutscher Taschenbuch Verlag München 1970.

L. Klinkhammer, *Zwischen Bündnis und Besatzung*, Niemeyer Tübingen 1993.

Ch. Maechling, *Pearl Harbor- The First Energy War*, in History Today dec. 2000.

B. Martin, *Deutschland und Japan im Zweiten Weltkrieg*, Musterschmidt Verlag Göttingen 1969.

W. Michalka (red.), *Nationalsozialistische Aussenpolitik*, Wissenschaftliche Buchgesellschaft Darmstadt 1978.

J.W. Morley, *Deterrent Diplomacy-Japan, Germany and the USSR 1935-1940*, Columbia University Press New York 1976.

M. Mourin, *Ciano contra Mussolini*, Prisma Boeken Utrecht 1963.

S. K. Pavlovitch, *History of the Balkans 1804-1945*, Longman London 1999.

P. Pierik, *Hungary 1944-1945*, Aspekt Nieuwegein 1998.

J. Pinckney Harrison, *The Long March to Power*, Mac Millan London 1972.

E. L. Presseisen, *Germany and Japan-A Study in Totalitarian Diplomacy*, Martinus Nijhoff Den Haag 1958.

R. Rahn, *Ruheloses Leben*, Diederichs Verlag Düsseldorf 1949.

G. Roberts, *Unholy Alliance*, J. B. Tauris London 1989.

M. Ros, *Jakhalzen van het Derde Rijk*, Arbeiderspers Amsterdam 1996.

D.E. Schüddekopf, *Nationalbolschewismus in Deutschland 1918-1933*, Ullstein Frankfurt 1973.

J. M. Siebert, *Italiens Weg in den Zweiten Weltkrieg*, Athenäum Verlag Frankfurt 1962.

E. Snow, *Red Star over China*, Gollancz Ltd London 1946.

Th. Sommer, *Deutschland und Japan zwischen den Mächten 1935-1940*, Siebeck Tübingen 1962.

A. Stam, *Stalins 'irredentisme'*, in Tweede Bulletin van de Tweede Wereldoorlog, Aspekt Soesterberg 2000.

L. Sütö, *La politique interalliée et la Hongrie pendant la Seconde Guerre Mondiale*, thesis Utrecht University 1983.

Sh. Togo, *Japan im Zweiten Weltkrieg*, Athenäum Verlag Bonn 1958.

G. R. Ueberschär, *Hitler und Finnland 1939-1941*, Steiner Wiesbaden 1978.

H. E. Volkmann, *Das Ruslandbild im Dritten Reich*, Böhlau Cologne 1994.

B. Wegner, *Hitler, der Zweite Weltkrieg und die Choreographie des Untergangs*, in Geschichte und Gesellschaft vol. 26 nr. 3 july 2000.

G. L. Weinberg, *Germany, Hitler and World war II*, Cambridge University Press New York 1995.

P. Weizler, *Hirohito and War*, University of Hawai Press Honolulu 2000.

Register

ABCD-States 63, 70
Abe 40
Abyssinia 23
Afghanistan 76
Albania 54, 55, 58
Amau Declaration 28
Ambrosio 93, 94
Amur 35
Anschluss 25, 33
Anti-Comintern Pact 7, 8, 16, 18, 19, 25, 30, 32, 35, 38, 39, 42, 51, 66-68, 102
Antonescu, Marshall 54, 60, 61, 64, 66, 67, 84, 85, 89, 92, 93, 98-100
Antonescu, Mihai 89, 90, 92, 99
Antwerp 45
Araki 14
Arctic 62
Arita 39, 40
Arrow Cross 102
Asahi Shimbun 39
Attollico 40, 43
Auriti 43
Austria 23, 25
Axis 63, 92

Badoglio 94-96
Balkan 25
Balkan Campaign 58
Baltic States 37, 51
Barbarossa, Operation 58, 59, 64, 66, 67, 77, 81, 83

Bardossy 64
Bastianini 92
Bauer, Colonel 26
Belo Russia 37
Berlin 34, 40, 50, 59
Bessarabia 37, 51, 65
Bloch 67
Blomberg 15, 30, 31
Bolshevism 16, 42, 64, 65
Bose, Subhas Chandra 76, 79
Bratianu 99
Brenner Pass 23, 46
Brest Litovsk, Peace of 88
Briand-Kellogg Treaty 30, 40
British Empire 44
British India 17, 77, 79
Brussels 31
Bucharest 90
Budapest 97, 98, 102
Bukovina 51, 52, 56, 65
Bulgaria 53, 56, 57, 67, 68, 80, 86, 99
Burma Road 48

Cairo 99
Carol, King 54
Caucasus 67
Chang Hsueh-liang 13, 14, 29
Changkufeng 36
Chang-Tso-lin 12, 13
Chiang-Kai shek 26-29, 31, 47
China 8, 10, 12, 25-29, 32, 35, 48, 75
'China Incident' 75
Chinese Civil War 27
Chunking 47
Ciano 25, 33-35, 41-43, 45, 52, 63, 78, 88, 90
Cold war 102
Comintern 18, 24
Communism 25, 87
Coox, Alvin 35
Croatia 58, 65, 67, 93, 96
Czechoslovakia 26, 33, 52

Dalmatia 58
Danube 54
Dardanelles 56
Denmark 66
Dirksen, Von 19, 43
Dobrudzha 99
Dolfuss 23
Dutch East Indies 47, 49, 63, 70, 79

El Salvador 32
Epirus 54
Ethiopia 23

Falkenhausen, Von 27
Fascism 25, 42, 94
Feltre 93
Finland 37, 42, 44, 52, 56, 56, 59, 66, 77, 78, 88, 103
France 23-25, 33, 37, 43, 47, 48, 51, 52, 90
Frick 17

Garda Lake 95
Germany 7, 8, 16, 24, 26, 32, 33, 35, 37, 38, 42, 44, 45, 49, 66, 75, 76, 79, 80, 85, 89, 90, 92, 102
Gestapo 101
Goebbels 81, 104
Grandi 94
Great Britain 8, 23, 33, 37, 43, 47, 56, 73, 78, 86
'Great East Asia' 49
Great Fascist Council 94
Greece 33, 54, 58, 86

Hamaguchi 10
Hanko 62
Hassell, Von 44, 79
Haushofer, Albrecht 25
Hawaï 49
Himmler 60
Hirohito 9, 13, 32, 66
Hitchins 66
Hitler 8, 15-17, 19, 24, 25, 32-34, 38, 40, 44, 46, 51, 58-61, 63, 67-69, 73-75, 78, 81, 84, 88, 90, 92, 93, 95, 97-99, 105, 106
Hojo 13
Horthy 60, 77, 84, 93, 98, 101
Hull, Cordell 47, 70, 74
Hungary 32, 52, 53, 57, 60, 64, 77, 85, 91-93, 97-99, 101, 102

Indelli 71
Indochina 48
Inner Mongolia 21, 29
Inuhai 14
Iron Guard 60, 89
Italy 7, 24, 25, 32, 33, 40, 42, 44, 45, 50, 55, 57, 74, 76, 88, 90, 95

Japan 7-11, 15-17, 18, 24, 25, 29, 30, 31, 35-38, 49, 55, 68, 73-75, 78, 79, 83, 104

Japanese-Chinese War 8, 30, 75
Jelavich 65
Jews 16, 60, 87, 98, 102

Kaganovich 45
Kallay 89, 92, 96, 98
Kilia 54
Klessheim 92, 93, 98
Komoto 12, 13
Konoye 30, 62, 63, 70, 81
Korea 13, 30, 36
Kretschmer 104
Kriegel 26
Kuomingtang 26, 27, 30, 47, 84
Kwantung 12
Kwantung Army 12-14, 21, 36, 83, 84

Laval 23
League of Nations 9, 15, 23, 29, 57
'Lebensraum' 14, 44
Leningrad 62
Liaotung 12
Litvinov 36
Locarno, Treaty of 24
London 37
london, Treaty of 10
'Long March' 27
Lytton report 15
Lyuskov 35

Macedonia 58, 86
Malacca 78
Malaysia 78, 79
Manchukuo 8, 14, 21, 29, 36, 57, 59
Manchuria 9, 12-15
Mannerheim 87, 103
Marco Polo Bridge 30
Matsuoka 49, 58, 59, 62
'Mein Kampf' 16
Michael, King 101
Middle East 67
Midway Islands 82
Molotov 55, 56

Mongolian People's Republic 8, 21, 22, 29 36, 38, 59
Moscow 35, 40, 43, 59, 81
Mozart Festival 74
Munich 47
Munich, Conference of 26, 33, 37
Mushakoji 19, 31
Mussolini 23, 25, 26, 33, 34, 42-47, 50, 63, 64, 68, 74, 78, 81, 83, 88, 90, 92-95

Nanu 99
Naples 94
Nazi Regime 49
Netherlands 48
Neurath, Von 15, 18, 31
Nice 41
Nine Power Pact 10, 31
Nomonhan 36, 85
Nomura, Admiral 70
Non Intervention 24
Nordic Race 16
North Africa 46, 47, 67, 82, 88
Norway 88, 104

Oil Embargo 70
'OKW' 31
'Open Door' 31
Oshima 17-19, 38, 39, 68, 73, 74, 82, 104
Ott 43, 71, 73, 74, 82, 84
Outer Mongolia 21

Pacific 74
Paris 37
Paul, Regent 57
Pearl Harbor 8, 9, 60, 75, 77
Petsamo 78
Philippines 73
Poland 8, 32, 33, 35, 37, 40, 42-44, 52
Popular Front 24
Portugal 90
Poznan 42

Pravda 51
Pruth 61, 99
Pu Yi 14

Raeder, Admiraal 81
Rahn 95, 98
Raumer, Von 18, 19
Red Army 35-37, 99, 103
Reichswehr 17, 26
Rhineland 24
Ribbentrop 17-19, 32-35, 38, 39, 44, 49, 51, 52, 55, 56, 59, 62, 67 73, 74, 81, 84, 93, 95, 103
Rintelen, Von 88
Romania 51-54, 58, 59, 64, 67, 85, 90-92, 96, 97, 100-102
Rome 45, 46, 95, 98
Roosevelt 46
Ros, Martin 60
Rotterdam 45
Russia 10, 37, 42, 44, 45, 68, 78
Ruthenia 57
Ryti 61

Salerno 94
Salo, Republic of 95, 96
Sanatescu 99
Sato 82
Savoy 41
Schnurre 61
Schulenberg, Von der 51, 56
Scoppa, Bova 90
Seeckt, Von 26
Serbia 86
Shigemitsu 36, 104
Shiratori 38
Siam 15
Siberia 10, 76
Sima, Horia 60, 61, 89, 100
Simovich 57
Singapore 68, 69
Slovakia 26, 57, 67, 93, 96
Slovenia 58
Smetanin 81

Sorge 83, 84
Southeast Asia 51, 63, 69, 78, 79
South Manchurian Railroad 12, 13
Soviet Union = USSR
Spain 19, 31, 43, 46, 55, 90
Spanish Civil War 24, 25
Stahmer 49, 51, 84, 103-105
Stalin 36, 37, 59, 82, 83, 88, 104
Stalingrad 86, 88
Stalin-Hitler Pact 35, 42, 62
Stimson Doctrine 14
Stirbey, Barbu 99
Sudetenland 26, 33
Suez Canal 24
Sugijama 71, 80
Szalási 102
Sztojay 64, 65, 98, 101

Tanaka 12
Tanner 45
Tatekawa 81
Thailand 15, 32
Third Reich 15, 20, 47, 50, 52, 66, 80, 102
Thomsen 73
Togo 70, 73, 74, 80, 81
Tojo 30, 70
Tokyo 17, 29, 49, 51, 104
Transnistria 65, 66
Trans Siberian Railroad 71
Transylvania 54, 65, 66, 85, 98, 100, 101
Trianon, Peace of 62
Tripartite Pact 8, 47, 49-51, 57, 66, 68, 71, 73, 77, 79, 92, 96, 102, 103
Tsuji 82
Tunesia 41, 93

Ukraine 37, 98, 104
United States 8, 10, 11, 18, 28, 44, 47-49, 71, 73, 82, 86

Usami 39
USSR 7, 8, 18, 20-22, 24, 26, 35, 36, 38, 39, 41, 52, 56, 62-64, 67, 69, 79, 83, 89, 103

Veesenmayer 98
Venice 23
Victor Emanuel III 94
Vienna Arbitration 53
Vietnam 70
Vladivostok 10, 11, 68, 74
Volga 89

Wang Ching-wei 47, 67, 68
Warsaw 42
Washington 15, 50 74
Wegner 87, 105, 106
Wehrmacht 18
Weiszäcker, Von 30, 39
Welles, Sumner 46
Wenneker, Admiral 73, 81, 84, 105
Wetzel 26
'Wiener Schiedsspruch' 53, 65, 100
Winter War 37, 61, 87
Woermann 39
World Revolution 45

Yugoslavia 27, 38, 58

Zeitzler 89
Zhukov 36